the VIRGIN MARY

© 2024 The American Society for the Defense of
Tradition, Family, and Property—TFP

All rights reserved. No part of this publication may be reproduced, distributed, or transmitted in any form or by any means, including photocopying, recording, or other electronic or mechanical methods, without the prior written permission of the publisher, except in the case of brief quotations embodied in critical reviews and other noncommercial uses permitted by copyright law. The American Society for the Defense of Tradition, Family, and Property—TFP is a registered name of The Foundation for a Christian Civilization Inc., a 501(c)(3) tax-exempt organization.
For permission requests, please write to:
The Foundation for a Christian Civilization, Inc.
1358 Jefferson Road, Spring Grove, Penn. 17362

Printed in the United States of America

To order more copies of this book, please contact:
America Needs Fatima
P.O. Box 341, Hanover, PA 17331
(888) 317-5571
ANF@ANF.org • www.ANF.org

the VIRGIN
MARY

by Father Raymond de Thomas de Saint-Laurent

Translated from the original French by Faustine Hillard

America Needs Fatima

Monument to the Immaculate Conception commissioned by Ferdinand II, King of the Two Sicilies, located at Piazza Mignanelli in Rome.

The Dogma of the Immaculate Conception was proclaimed by Pope Pius IX in the Apostolic Constitution *Ineffabilis Deus* on December 8, 1854:

"We declare, pronounce, and define that the doctrine which holds that the most Blessed Virgin Mary, in the first instance of her conception, by a singular grace and privilege granted by Almighty God, in view of the merits of Jesus Christ, the Savior of the human race, was preserved free from all stain of original sin, is a doctrine revealed by God and therefore to be believed firmly and constantly by all the faithful."

GO TO MARY.

There is no more direct route to Our Lord.

INTRODUCTION Our Life and Our Sweetness	vii
CHAPTER I The Immaculate Conception	1
CHAPTER II The Nativity of the Virgin Mary	8
CHAPTER III The Holy Name of Mary	15
CHAPTER IV Mary's Life in the Temple	23
CHAPTER V The Annunciation	31
CHAPTER VI The Divine Motherhood	38
CHAPTER VII The Visitation	45
CHAPTER VIII Mary's Sanctification	51
CHAPTER IX The Finding of Our Lord in the Temple	59
CHAPTER X The Blessed Virgin's Compassion	65
CHAPTER XI Mary's Death and the Assumption	73
NOTES	81

INTRODUCTION
Our Life and Our Sweetness

When the Blessed Virgin enters into the life of a soul, she causes a radiant springtime to blossom there. She chases away gloomy clouds of sadness, doubt, and discouragement. Hearts that give themselves sincerely to her are flooded with clarity, peace, and happiness.

Would you like to transform your life? Would you like to practice easily those virtues God asks of you and yet seem so inaccessible? Would you like to know the indescribable joys that only the love of Jesus can obtain, and which have caused the delight of saints? Would you like to experience these marvels yourself?

If you sincerely desire this, do not hesitate a second: Go to Mary. There is no more direct route to Our Lord.

In these few pages, we propose to study the radiant figure of the Immaculate Mother. By following her through the main phases of her life, we can learn to know her better and thus love her with greater tenderness, invoke her with greater confidence, and serve her with greater fidelity. In so doing, we will have efficaciously progressed toward the salvation of our own souls, for devotion to Our Lady is one of the surest signs of predestination.

Mary, as we chant in the Divine Office, is our life and our sweetness—*"Vita, dulcedo et spes nostra, salve!"* These consoling and profound words will serve as a dogmatic introduction to this modest volume and will recall the important role that the Mother of Christ plays in each of our lives.

It is true that heretics are scandalized at the cult with

which we honor the Blessed Virgin. "How dare you call Mary 'your life'!" they exclaim. "Jesus alone is the life of souls. He declared this solemnly at the Last Supper: when He said 'I am the way, the truth and the life; no one comes to the Father except through Me.'[1] The Savior did love His mother but never offered her such exaggerated praise. . ." Such is the great objection of the Protestants.

We answer by boldly proclaiming what Our Lord did for us. He took on a body like ours to win our hearts and become our companion and friend. He led a life of labor and obscurity for nearly thirty years to encourage us by His divine example. He revealed eternal truths to enlighten our darkened minds. Undergoing the horrible tortures of the Passion, He suffered and died in expiation for our sins. Finally, He hid Himself under the Eucharistic veil to render Himself as food for our souls and the faithful companion of our exile here below.

Jesus certainly is the life of our wretched hearts. Remove from our Religion the Gospel that instructs us, the sacrament of Penance that returns us to life, and the Eucharist that feeds us, and nothing would be left. Indeed, we would languish in desperation in the shadow of death.

Yet this abundant and divine life the Savior brings us is bestowed upon us only through Mary. The Messiah could have come to earth as Adam did—in the fullness of His strength and beauty. Nothing would have been easier for the Almighty! Instead, He chose to be born of a Virgin. Indeed, Mary formed His divine body in her immaculate womb. It was she who fed and watched over Him during His first years, keeping Him near her for a long time. When the hour of her supreme immolation had arrived, she stood at the foot of the cross. With her wholly agonized soul, she offered to the Father His beloved Son for the salvation of mankind. It is Mary who gives Jesus to the world.

The sublime role of the Virgin Mother continues. Our Lord is not merely content with coming into the world in the grotto of Bethlehem. He actually desires to be born in each of our souls. When we receive sanctifying grace, the life of Christ is born within us. However, Our Lord is not to be born in our hearts only to die soon after! He wishes to grow and take form in our innermost being. This happens when we progress in virtue. This mysterious birth and growth of Our Lord within us is the work of the Virgin Mary. No Catholic should have the slightest doubt about this. Our Lady is she who bestows the graces the Savior merited for us by His precious blood. All favors from heaven come to us through her hands: Such is the unanimous teaching of Catholic Tradition.

Is your heart unsteady? Amid the violent temptations of the world, do you endure great difficulty in safeguarding the treasure of divine friendship within your heart? Despite good resolutions, do you repeatedly fail to follow God's graces? If so, do not hesitate. You are too far from the source of grace and have not called upon Mary's aid. Had you called upon her more readily, you would not have fallen.

Is your heart discouraged by the trials which trouble you? What do you do at the hour of tribulation? Do you give in to despair? In times of difficulty, do you forget to pray, or neglect your exercises of piety? You would be better off to throw yourself instinctively into the arms of your heavenly Mother and to pray to her at all cost. When you feel that you no longer have the strength to murmur a simple Hail Mary, call out to her by her blessed name. At that very moment, she will cover you with her mantle, console, and comfort you.

Mary is the life of our souls because she gives us Jesus, the Author of all life.

* * *

She is also our sweetness. She is not content merely with working efficaciously for our salvation; indeed she finds ways to make it easier. With the tenderness of a mother, she strews flowers on the difficult path of virtue we walk. She did not forget Our Lord's final words addressed to her from the cross. While agonizing, He entrusted us to her care. Referring to each one of us, He said to her: "Woman behold thy son."[2] These words engraved themselves deeply in the Virgin's heart, so pure and good. Ever since then, this most loving of mothers unceasingly fulfills her duties to us, her children.

In fact, the Mother of God is well aware that she is somewhat indebted to us for the immense privileges she has received. Would she have known the joys of Divine Motherhood had we not sinned, had we not needed the Redemption, joys which by far surpass our weak minds? In this manner, it is with a kind of gratitude that she stoops to help us in our suffering.

How does the Holy Virgin sweeten our lives? She intercedes with Our Lord to ward off the pains and punishment we so often merit. As at the wedding feast of Cana, she is moved by our distress and compassionately intercedes for us to her divine Son. The tender heart of Christ is often moved by her prayers.

There are times when trials arise in our lives, for suffering is the great law of life. Mary obtains such an abundance of grace for all those who call upon her that they do not feel the burden that weighs upon them.

How can one even doubt that divine consolations can alleviate the sting of suffering? Read the story of the Japanese martyrs who sang canticles while the flames of the pyre devoured them. They experienced ineffable joy in the midst of torment; their souls ascended to heaven rejoicing.

In your troubles, cast upon Mary a prolonged look of hope and love. Learn from your own experience what the great servants of Our Lady have so often felt. Yes, crosses are often bitter, but as Saint Louis de Montfort used to say, our divine Mother steeps them in the honey of divine charity.[3]

CHAPTER I
The Immaculate Conception

When Garcia Moreno[4] fell under the blows of the assassins who struck him down out of hatred for religion, a last flicker of light shone in his eyes as he murmured: "God does not die." This is an extremely magnificent declaration of faith and hope. Truly, the Almighty cannot be vanquished!

Yet by choosing to manifest His abundant love through the work of Creation, it seems that the Lord suffered failure after failure. He created the angels to be companions of His infinite delights, yet many of them preferred to indulge their pride rather than enjoy the beatific joys of divine love.

He created our first parents for a happiness that far exceeds the most demanding expectations of the human heart. Yet they turned away from their Sovereign Benefactor out of ingratitude.

The Lord could not suffer what seemed to be a "double defeat." Rather, He deserved a brilliant restitution. The incomparable Artist returned to work, conceiving the idea of an admirable creature whose beauty would far surpass man in the brilliance of his original innocence, and whose radiant perfection would outshine the light of the most splendid angels. When the time was fulfilled, He completed this masterpiece of His intelligence and love: He created the Virgin Mary.

The first privilege accorded her was her Immaculate Conception.

We must fully understand what this unique privilege means.

With the conception of Mary, the Most High did more than just condescend to obey the universal laws governing the coming of men into the world. He did not form Our Lady miraculously by virtue of the Holy Ghost as was later done with her divine Son. Indeed, she had both a father and a mother. But the Lord, Who from all eternity had chosen Joachim and Anne to give life to the Queen of Heaven, had raised them to a great degree of holiness. Their noble mission places them so much higher than the other Saints that they undoubtedly deserve special homage. We are too often unmindful of this, yet we could benefit by recognizing their sanctity, for these two great souls enjoy a powerful influence over the heart of their beloved daughter.

The privilege of the Immaculate Conception consists in Mary's exemption from the fatal inheritance we carry into the world at birth. The same moment that gives life to our bodies gives death to our souls. We are born children of wrath— *"natura filii irae."*[5] Throughout our fleeting lives, we endure the heavy burden resulting from the fall of Adam. Allowing ourselves to be seduced by error, we lack the self-mastery to resist the temptations that challenge us. Our corrupted flesh is seared by the abominable fire of concupiscence. Our hearts are rent by affliction, our bodies tortured by sickness. Finally, hideous death overcomes us—and we must suffer the supreme ignominy of the putrefaction that consumes our corpse and the worms that vie with one another for our remains! How the curse from heaven due to Adam's sin oppresses us! How understandable is the cry of anguish uttered by Job in his misery: "Let the day perish wherein I was born."[6]

On the contrary, many, many times blessed was the day the Queen of Heaven was conceived! From the solemn mo-

THE IMMACULATE CONCEPTION 3

ment when Our Lord created her soul and united it with her small virginal body, He made it, by the work of His powerful hands, to emerge all white, all radiant, all pure. Not a single minute, not a single second, not a single infinitesimal fraction of a second was this magnificent soul sullied by the stain of original sin. Not even for an infinitesimal fraction of a second could the serpent glare at Mary with a look of hate-

Madonna del Miracolo. Painting in the Church of Sant' Andrea delle Fratte, Rome.

ful pride nor covet her as his prey. Seeing this, the serpent recognized with overwhelming anger that the woman who had been promised had come, the immaculate one who would crush his head with her virginal heel.

Since Mary was preserved from original sin, it logically follows that she would not be subject to the consequences of that sin. Let us then contemplate how this is reflected in her virginal soul. No narrow-mindedness limited her intelligence, for hers was the most wise, penetrating, and enlightened intellect after that of Our Lord. No weakness impaired her will, the most vigorous and ardent will ever created. No selfishness restricted her heart, the most all-encompassing, generous, and caring heart ever known after that of her Son.

This glory of her Immaculate Conception was reflected in her body. She did not experience the concupiscence that wreaks such havoc within us. Sickness did not harm her. Finally, unlike the rest of men, Our Lady was subject to neither pain nor bodily death. Nevertheless, God willed that she experience both suffering and death that she might know the same torments we suffer. With this store of shared experience, Our Lady's compassion for us is all the more maternal and merciful.

We have so far studied only a small part of this great mystery. The Almighty did much more than create Mary in a state of grace like that of the angels and our first parents. He graced her soul with the sum of all virtues to such an imminent degree that our minds cannot grasp its splendor. Theologians teach that from that first moment, the Blessed Virgin surpassed in perfection not only the highest angel, but all angels and saints put together.

Her incomparable beauty is such that the Holy Ghost exclaims in admiration: "Thou art all beautiful, O my love, and there is no blemish in thee"—*Tota pulchra es et macula non est in te.*[7]

* * *

When Pope Pius IX defined the dogma of the Immaculate Conception, the Catholic world cried out with joy. The cannons of Castel Sant'Angelo, where the pontifical flag still waved in Rome's brilliant light, fired and announced the glad news to the world. All over the world, the faithful proclaimed their joy. In many big cities, homes were spontaneously decked with banners and illuminated with candles and lanterns.

Christian hearts understandably rejoiced in seeing another flower of glory adorn the crown of their Mother. Does this privilege of the Virgin Mary, however, communicate the same kind of moral well-being to our souls? Does it not rather elevate Our Lady to such great heights that she appears even farther removed from our misery? Quite the contrary! Our Catholic consciences would be poorly schooled indeed if we did not find the Immaculate Conception of Mary as the very basis for her virtually infinite goodness.

All men are endowed with a fundamental generosity rendering them at certain times capable of the most admirable self-sacrifice. Those who survived battles can testify to the unfathomable heroism that can spring forth from the human soul. Indeed, how many young people have requested dangerous missions in the place of their older comrades? They knew the dangers involved yet proceeded to their deaths with smiles on their lips. They believed their sacrifice would deliver a father whose small children were also smiling in the distant purity of their cribs.

Unfortunately, many obstacles prevent the full maturing of such natural generosity, a magnificent vestige of our original state of beauty. We know these obstacles all too well from personal experience. Are our hearts not moved at the sight of another's distress? Yet does not the bitter voice of self-interest all too often cover up the instinctive response which springs from the heart? Are we not often insensitive to our neighbor's suffering because of our love of comfort and pleasure? Our selfishness paralyses and often completely stifles the goodness of our hearts.

The Queen of Heaven knows no such pettiness! No selfishness can prevent her from merciful gestures of compassion and tenderness toward her children.

There is more. God formed the soul of Mary as the most faithful image of His adorable perfections. God's infinite goodness causes Him to fill us with more and more abundant blessings; indeed, this led the Incarnate Word to the supreme folly of the cross. Like her Son, the Blessed Virgin carries within her heart a ceaselessly burning fire of love for us. She would gladly sacrifice her life a thousand times over for our benefit. Since she is a mere creature, her suffering on Calvary did not have infinite value like that of Jesus, but it did almost equal in intensity that of the Savior. That she did not die of sorrow at the foot of the cross is, in fact, a veritable miracle.

Does it not seem that Our Lady herself wanted to explain to us the relationship between her original purity and her goodness? Recall the miraculous grotto at Lourdes on the banks of the Gave, where she established the throne of her mercy. Prodigies occur without ceasing. How did the pure lady of the apparition answer when Bernadette asked her name? Joining her hands, her countenance lit with a most luminous smile, and lifting her eyes to heaven, she said with an expression of ineffable gratitude, "I am the Immaculate Conception." Speaking thus, she implicitly told us: "Let us join together in thanking the Most High for having preserved me from original sin. Since I am all pure, I am also all good."

* * *

May these considerations inspire you to a practical and unshakable faith in Mary's goodness. With Saint Bernard, believe firmly that you will never invoke our Heavenly Mother in vain. Confide the desires of your soul to her. She will fortify you in your temptations and give you a small spark of her love for Jesus. This spark will enkindle the sweet fire of divine charity in your soul. Confide the cares of your heart to her. Are you hurt by moments of ingratitude or scorn, which can be so especially cruel when coming from the persons you love? Are you broken by sorrows that suddenly extinguish the joy of your meager existence? Tell Mary your troubles; she will console you, and your tears of grief will turn into tears of gratitude.

Confide your material cares to her. She will arrange everything according to your true best interests. In all of your difficulties, in every circumstance, at every moment, look to the gentle Star of the Sea, invoke Mary!— *"Respice stellum, voca Mariam."*[8]

CHAPTER II
The Nativity of the Virgin Mary

Many days passed before God finally completed the masterpiece of His creation. For nine months, the soul of Mary had given form to her virginal body, and the hour of her happy birth approached. As the suffocating Palestinian summer neared its end, the mellowing sun poured abundant torrents of golden light on the opulent plain of Samaria, ripening the rich orchards of autumn fruit. On a magnificent September day, with nature adorned in radiant beauty, the most Holy Virgin came into the world in the white-walled city of Nazareth.

She was probably born in the same house where the great mystery of the Incarnation later took place and where Jesus spent most of His childhood and youth in work and prayer. The angels did not acclaim the coming of the glorious Queen with hymns of joy as they later did the birth of the Savior. Invisible to the eyes of mortal men, the angels considered it an honor to mount guard around the humble crib over which Saints Joachim and Anne lovingly watched. The prophecy of Isaiah had come to pass. The root of Jesse, ten centuries removed, had sprouted a new branch. On this same branch in but a few years more would blossom the eternal Flower, the Incarnate Word.

Her divine Son would soon appear representing a new dawn of hope upon a world plunged for four thousand years into the darkness of pain and death.

THE NATIVITY OF THE VIRGIN MARY

The day the Queen of Heaven was born ranks as one of the most beautiful in history since it announced to condemned mankind the long-awaited time of liberation. In commemorating this great event, the Church bursts forth in its enthusiasm: "Thy nativity, O Virgin Mother of God," sings the Church in its liturgy, "has announced joy to the whole world"—*Nativitas tua, Dei Genitrix Virgo, gaudium annuntiavit universo mundo.*[9]

Indeed, we seem to forget in what horrible distress the world lay prostrate before the coming of Christ.

The sin of our first parents had borne the fruit of death. Until the coming of the Savior, the curse of the Almighty lay heavily upon sinful humanity. Adam had eaten of the forbidden fruit in the wild hope of becoming like God. With terrible irony, God stripped him of his magnificent privileges and reduced him to extreme misery. Thus, the ancient world was founded upon oppression of the weak and disregard for human dignity. The greater part of mankind was subject to the torments of slavery. Even Rome, the proud bearer of civilization, considered the multitude of its slaves as but an immense herd destined for slaughter. Indeed, masters had the power to send their slaves to their deaths solely to amuse themselves. The refined patricians of the Imperial City would sometimes use these poor souls as fod-

Saint Anne teaching the Virgin Mary. Statue in the Church of the Gesù, Rome.

der for the salt-water eels they raised. Nothing satisfied their gluttony more than these delicious marine eels, fattened on human blood.

The distress of souls was even more acute. Adam had supposed that he could do without God. He unappreciatively spurned his Sovereign Benefactor. God, in return, withdrew from His creature. He did not abandon mankind altogether, however, but spoke to him at rare intervals, announcing the future coming of a virgin who would crush the head of the serpent under her immaculate heel. He raised up prophets from among the people, yet He hid Himself within His inaccessible light.

Moreover, the Lord had not allowed the source of grace to cease entirely. He did not refuse His pardon to the repen-

The Virgin Child at Prayer, by Francisco de Zurbarán. Prado Museum, Madrid.

tant sinner, granting it under the sole condition of a perfect contrition. Even so, amid the temptations of the flesh and deprived of the abundant spiritual help now available to us, the weakest souls fell by the thousands into the infernal pit.

Poor men of ancient times! They keenly sensed their weakness and vulnerability, and they searched in intense anguish for some way to gain supernatural assistance in their necessity. God, a spiritual Being, escapes man's rude senses, so men made idols in which to place their utmost hope. Alas, these statues were deaf and did not hear the heartrending cries arising from forty centuries of distress.

Yet, this terrible nightmare wherein mankind struggles dissipates like a dense nocturnal fog before the sweet morning light. The quadrant of eternity marks the hour of its infinite mercy. The birth of Mary begins the work of Redemption. In her crib, the mother of the Savior illuminates the desolate earth with the grace of her first smiles. Jesus will soon appear and, with His precious blood, will erase the sentence of our condemnation. The world which has suffered so, will finally delight in the joy of liberty and peace. Slavery will everywhere be abolished, and human dignity will henceforth be respected. Like a flowing stream, graces will spring forth in abundance from the sacraments. We have but to approach and draw from them—without limit—pardon, courage, and life everlasting.

The God who hid in Paradise will descend to earth and never abandon mankind. After His Ascension, Our Lord will remain among us under the Eucharistic veil until the end of time, when the Real Presence will leave the destroyed tabernacles. Christ will then visibly reign over the glorious souls of the resurrected elect. Such are the great joys the birth of Mary announces. "Thy nativity, O Virgin Mother of God has announced joy to the whole world."

The birth of the Blessed Virgin was, then, one of the foremost events of history. Let us now examine how the birth was received and draw lessons from this meditation that will benefit our interior lives.

The holy Fathers of the Church express the impact of the birth of the Immaculate Virgin on the invisible world by describing the heavens overwhelmed with wondrous admiration. The angels were at a loss to find adequate praises for acclaiming the adorable Trinity for having created her who was the beloved Daughter of the Father, and who would become the Mother of the Word Incarnate and the Spouse of the Holy Ghost. Nor did they weary of admiring the beauties of their queen. The blessed spirits, who rejoice at the conversion of a single soul, rejoiced upon seeing the appearance of the sure Refuge of sinners. They knew that Mary would one day be the Gate of Heaven who would never refuse entry into the eternal kingdom to those who invoked her with confidence.

The Fathers also note the immense sigh of relief of the just in limbo, those who had died since the beginnings of the world, as well as the furor of the demons in Hell, who saw the approaching end of their tyrannical reign.

How was the birth of Mary, which delighted heaven and terrified the fallen angels, received on earth? The birth of Saint John the Baptist several years later was accompanied by miracles that vividly impressed the popular imagination. The inhabitants of Judea asked themselves with admiration: "What will become of this child whose arrival in this world is hailed by so many prodigies? What, then, will this child be?"[10] The sublime mission of Mary far surpassed that of the Precursor. Yet, nothing extraordinary indicated to the multitudes that she who was promised to sinful man immediately after the fall and whom the prophets had announced throughout the centuries was born. In fact, the Immaculate Virgin was born amid universal indifference.

According to certain traditions, no one in the small town of Nazareth where Saints Joachim and Anne lived paid heed to the new arrival. Although the blood of David flowed in her veins, her family had fallen from its ancient splendor. Who noticed these impoverished people?

Anne and Joachim had been childless for many years, but the Lord had at last answered their prayers. They saw their daughter Mary as the measure of His celestial goodness to them. Little did they suspect, however, the veritable treasures the Most High had instilled in the soul of their child. They could not have imagined the wonder of her Immaculate Conception. They did not realize that the Mother of the Redeemer lay in their loving arms.

The Jews of the time were plunged in discouragement. The voice of the prophets had not been heard for years. Having lost their political freedom, they believed Providence had abandoned them. It was then that the hidden work of infinite Mercy began to be accomplished in their midst.

These facts speak for themselves and teach us an obvious lesson. Would that the obscurity of Our Lady's birth teach us to make little of human greatness! Let us keep a Christian perspective of indifference toward the fleeting vanities that Christ Himself shunned in His Mother's birth. Were these important, surely He would not have refused them to His mother.

This great mystery also teaches us never to lose heart. The Immaculate Mother came into the world at a time when the Jews had lost hope. Indeed, they thought all was lost. Let us reap the benefit of this lesson. We often become discouraged when, calling on heaven to assist us, our request is not immediately granted. Sometimes God waits until we are on the brink of the abyss before extending His hand of mercy. So, let us not become discouraged and cease praying! The Almighty will intervene at the very moment when we believe ourselves completely abandoned. If we have confidence—an unlimited supply of confidence—we will be greatly rewarded!

* * *

Saint Thomas of Villanova explained in a sermon that Mary is the heavenly dawn, not only for the world, but especially for each individual soul. He recalled the great truth taught by Catholic tradition that a soul imbued with devotion to the Blessed Virgin carries within it the sign of predestination. Do you firmly desire to be saved from final damnation? Then faithfully honor Mary. Do you wish to guarantee the salvation of those who are dear to you? Obtain from them the promise that they not fail to recite some prayer to Mary every day. Catholic Tradition states that a servant of Our Lady cannot perish: "*Servus Mariae non peribit.*" He will forever sing the mercy of Jesus and of His holy Mother.

CHAPTER III
The Holy Name of Mary

Eight days after the birth of the Immaculate Virgin, her father and mother gathered their family and relatives into their humble dwelling. According to Jewish custom, they were to name the child that Heaven had granted them.

Although God chose to perform no external prodigies to mark the Blessed Virgin's entrance into the world, He had chosen, from all eternity, the noble name the Mother of the Savior was to bear. Thus, while Joachim and Anne awaited the fulfillment of their hopes with joyful impatience, the Archangel Gabriel, the great messenger of infinite mercy, visited them, revealing the blessed name the Most High Himself had reserved for their daughter.

Therefore, family deliberations around the crib where the Queen of Heaven lay smiling were not prolonged. Without hesitation, the parents of the Blessed Virgin confirmed they would name their child "Mary." We shall now meditate upon the profound meanings God veiled under so sweet a name.

* * *

The most renowned commentators teach that the name Mary means, first of all, "sovereign one." Indeed, the Immaculate Virgin reigns gloriously over the earth by the homage we render her and in Heaven by the splendor of her power and beauty. Her divine Son willed that all creation be entirely

Our Lady of Hope of Macarena. American TFP headquaters, Spring Grove, PA.

subject to her scepter of love.

Consider, however, what a strange contrast there is between her role as incomparable Queen and that of her life on earth. Does she not seem to unite two diametrically opposed tendencies? To the most obscure humility, God joined the most incomprehensible greatness.

Do not expect to find this sovereign in a magnificent palace, where innumerable servants wait to fulfill her slightest desire. Instead, she dwells in Nazareth in a small white house so lacking in amenities that today's poorest would disdain it. This narrow hovel, divided into two rooms of unequal dimensions, covered at the most a hundred and fifty square feet. There the Blessed Virgin dwelt with Joseph and Jesus—the eternal Son of God, and her son, the blessed fruit of her womb.

While the Savior planes heavy boards with His foster father, how does she who is blessed among all women spend her time? She occupies herself with the care of her meager household, cooking, washing, and mending clothes. This is truly an unusual sovereign—more like a humble servant girl than a great queen. Yet, in this modest work she displays so much love that the perfume of her tremendous virtue inebriates the heart of God. From on high, the angels incline in admiration to contemplate better the incomparable splendor before which their own glory pales.

There is more. We have seen with what treasures God filled the soul of Mary at the moment of her Immaculate Conception. Thereafter, the virgin grew so greatly and ceaselessly in grace and virtue from the very first moment of the use of her reason that our limited minds are awestruck. Moreover, Our Lord, who placed the crown of thaumaturge upon the heads of so many of His saints, undoubtedly granted His Mother the gift of miracles to the highest degree.

Nevertheless, during Our Lord's lifetime until His triumphant ascension into Heaven, the Blessed Virgin performed none of the prodigies that delight crowds. Jesus traveled throughout Palestine healing the sick and raising the dead. The Apostles, including Judas, expelled demons in the name of their Master. Yet Mary remained quietly in her simple house, save when she occasionally joined the crowds to hear her Son's preaching, where she was scarcely noticed among the attentive throngs. Thus we are witness to how profoundly hidden the Queen of Angels was from the eyes of men.

At the same time, Mary possesses the greatest authority ever over all the earth. During the days of Rome's empire, the Emperor commanded millions of men from the splendor of his palace. He scarcely knew the awesome number of his subjects: Europe obeyed his laws, and parts of Asia and Africa were subject to his scepter. On earth, Mary commanded but a single man, but a man greater than all kings, more glorious than all angels. This man is the God Who created the universe by the singular power of His infinite word. Because He is veritably her Son in the flesh, Jesus owes Mary—in strict justice—His respect, love, and obedience.

We have already recognized the Immaculate Conception of the Blessed Virgin as the foundation of her nearly infinite goodness. We now salute her divine Motherhood as the foundation of her scarcely limited power.

We know that God grants immense consideration to certain favored souls in heaven. Saint Thérèse of the Child Jesus, for example, announced on her deathbed that she would cause a shower of roses to fall upon the earth. Her gracious prediction is marvelously fulfilled every day in astonishing favors granted. If Our Lord accords such power to a simple nun, who died in the flower of her youth, what then would He not do for the highest, the most virtuous, the most beautiful of all His creatures, for the one who formed His divine body in her virginal womb?

We must profoundly engrave in our hearts this teaching, supported by the great voice of our Tradition: Jesus fulfills the least desire of His mother in Heaven as promptly as He fulfilled her requests upon earth. Our Lady wished to be represented on the miraculous medal with open hands, pouring out over the world, not a shower of roses, but torrents of grace, of light, of holy joy. If you want your prayer granted surely and rapidly, turn to the Immaculate Virgin.

* * *

The name of Mary also means "bitter." Announcing the future Messiah to the world, the prophet Isaiah called Him a "man of sorrows," *virum dolorum*.[11] Our Lady, the most perfect imitator of Our Lord, was the sorrowful Virgin, *Mater dolorosa*.

Suffering is the great element of redemption. By suffering, Mary united herself to the work of our deliverance at the foot of the cross. It is by accepting trials in a Christ-like manner that we find salvation. Finally, it is by suffering that we are able to obtain the grace of salvation for souls dear to us. Although this truth seems severe, it is less terrible than it first appears. While the infinitely merciful and good God sends us suffering, He always sends strength along with it and often includes consolation and great sweetness as well. In our lives, suffering is the mysterious messenger of true joy. The life of the Blessed Virgin strikingly illustrates this principle.

During the childhood of Jesus, Mary suffered unspeakable anguish. She saw Him born in a wretched stable and gave heed to the ominous prediction of the elderly Simeon. She was forced to flee to Egypt to guard her precious treasure from the murderous rage of Herod. She lost her child in Jerusalem, finding Him only after three long days of tears and agony. The horrible prophecy of Isaiah about the Messiah's tortures was continually present to her mind. Yet, what inexpressible consolations were hers! Her Son grew up sheltered by her motherly embrace. Sharing a profound intimacy, He illuminated her virginal soul with His divine smile and covered her with the most tender caresses of His divine love.

Mary suffered still more when Jesus had to leave the small house they shared for so many years to begin His public ministry. She was consoled to see Him often, however, and at times to witness His triumphs. The Master's voice, captivating the multitudes, also inspired the heart of the Virgin to blessed ecstasy.

On Calvary, Mary endured an unspeakable martyrdom.

She witnessed the same Son she had cared for with such devotion now crowned with thorns, bathed in blood, and nailed to a cross. She saw Him agonize and die, yet she was consoled by the conviction that His final victory would soon resound when He resurrected on the third day in His glorious body.

After her Son's Ascension, the Blessed Virgin felt a terrible longing for the daily affection she had shared with Him. She was consoled when Our Lord revealed and gave Himself to her in the Eucharist.

Then came the time of her sweet death.[12] The Immaculate Virgin was triumphantly taken into Heaven, like her Son, in her glorified body. The dreadful winter had run its course, and for her the springtime of eternity began.

What attitude should the Christian soul take when faced with suffering? We must accept it with faith and humility. Faith lets us see that suffering is a gift from God that allows us to reap great benefits when we make holy use of it. Humility lets us see how weak we are and that we would succumb, were it not for grace, under the weight of the trial. When God sends us suffering, let us ask Him for both the strength to withstand it and the profound consolations promised for all providential suffering.

Should we go still further? Should we desire trials? Should we seek them as for a special favor? Let us speak candidly.

Nowadays, there are certain pious works that lend themselves to a perilous exaggeration. These praise the advantages of suffering while forgetting that only the love of God is meritorious. They call upon souls to offer themselves as victims to the Most High. I recognize with the Church that there are times when God chooses particular souls to be victims for His Justice, but this is very rarely the case even among the saints. Actually, as long as Our Lord has not clearly manifested His will for a considerable time, none should think himself called to such exceptional trials. To act otherwise, spontaneously asking God for suffering, would be insane pride and foolish imprudence. Saint Francis de Sales, certainly an inspired director of souls, did not profess any other teaching than this. Therefore, let us sanctify ourselves in the fulfillment of our daily duties and let the Good Master send what best suits us.

* * *

Let us often invoke the name of Mary. God imparted such power to this blessed name that it works miracles, causing even demons to flee since they cannot hear it without being seized with alarm. The name of Mary dispels the most violent temptations and restores confidence and serenity to souls. In her revelation to Saint Bridget, Our Lady assured us that she herself would assist the faithful who frequently invoked her name during their lifetime.

When Saint John of God, who founded a religious order while yet in the flower of his youth, approached his end, he lay in his deathbed waiting to appear before the Sovereign Judge. After receiving the last sacraments, he hoped to be blessed with a visit of the Immaculate Virgin. When she failed to appear, the saint seemed discouraged. Agony had taken its toll when, suddenly, the face of the dying man was transformed. The Queen of Heaven appeared to him: "John," she said with a maternal smile, "do you think me capable of abandoning my devoted servants at such an hour?" Thus, in the embrace of the Virgin, he breathed his last.

CHAPTER IV
Mary's Life in the Temple

Saints Joachim and Anne proved their gratitude to God Who, against all hope, had satisfied their innermost desire. They promised, probably with a vow, to consecrate their daughter to the service of the Temple. Such a practice was nothing out of the ordinary for the chosen people of God. For generations, a given number of young girls would devote their lives from childhood until their wedding day in the House of the Lord. There they received the education commonly given to women of Israel in their day. Several passages of Holy Scripture refer to them spending their days praying and working. Indeed, they embroidered the fine linen and the sumptuous purple ornaments bordered with gold used in the liturgy. They enhanced the magnificence of the liturgical celebration with their singing. Finally, as the book of Kings tells us, they formed an honor guard before the Tabernacle.

When the Virgin Mary attained the age of three, her pious parents fulfilled their promise to the Lord. Despite the immense sorrow of losing their daughter, such a tender, gracious, and gentle child, they took her to Jerusalem. The Immaculate Virgin, who enjoyed use of her reason from the moment she was born, understood the significance of this act. On that day, she who had already been entirely consecrated to the Lord, gave herself fully to Him with all the élan of her will and love.

Her devotion, however, did not prevent her from acutely experiencing the bitterness of her sacrifice. As souls draw closer to God, they become more loving and good. Indeed, the affectionate heart of Mary was torn when she left her parents, but, even at such a young age, she ascended the long stairway to the Temple unhesitatingly and disappeared into the House of God.

* * *

For twelve years the Queen of Heaven dwelled in the shadow of the sanctuary, leading a hidden and very ordinary life. Let us bow respectfully before her and ask permission to draw near her soul that we might study her virtues in the Temple, which made her the favorite garden of the Most High.

How did the Blessed Virgin consider herself, she who was such an incomparable masterpiece of the Lord and the most beautiful of all creatures aside from the holy humanity of our Savior? Assuredly, Mary knew she had received exceptional favors. She sensed the absence of any interior temptation, the fire of love burning within her heart, and the incomparable and frequent ecstasies, without ever calling attention to herself. All this proved without a doubt the immensity of God's divine mercy for her.

In the Temple of Jerusalem, however, she was not aware of the grandeur that was hers. It seems unlikely that she would have known of the unique privilege of her Immaculate Conception. In any case, she was not cognizant that the Son of God had chosen from all eternity to take on flesh in her womb. She would have thought herself fortunate to have become the humble servant of this glorious virgin who would one day be the Mother of the Messiah. Little did she suspect the honor that awaited her.

Give heed to what she revealed to Saint Elizabeth of Hungary: "Be certain that I saw myself as the lowliest creature and most unworthy of God's graces."[13] Do not be astounded to hear such an affirmation! After Our Lord, only Mary understood more profoundly the immensity of the Most High and the lowliness of mankind. She knew that by her human nature she was nothing. She attributed the virtues adorning her heart to God alone, taking no merit for them whatsoever. In the presence of the Heavenly Father, she immersed herself in an unfathomable abyss of humility.

Her exterior manner reflected this humility. No other child showed herself more docile to her tutors. She learned much that she did not know through infused knowledge. She

was taught to read the Scriptures, to sew and embroider, and made rapid progress. The priests also taught her about divine things, although she was incomparably more advanced than they! Yet, she listened to their lessons with respectful attention and submitted in every way to their opinions.

The Virgin Mary's humility made her attentive and helpful toward her little companions. She revealed to Saint Mechtilde that as she immersed herself in the consideration of her nothingness, she liked to admire their youthful virtues. It never occurred to her to prefer herself over the least among them.

This rare humility enchanted the adorable Trinity. Indeed, it merited a sublime response, attracting the Incarnate Word to reside within Our Lady's chaste womb. If the Immaculate Virgin pleased the Most High by her spotless purity, said Saint Bernard, it was by her humility that she became the Mother of God: *"Virginitate placuit, humilitate concepti."*[14]

* * *

This study should not be merely speculative. It must have practical applications. Let us then speak with frank brutality and merciless cruelty. I pray this humble and gentle Virgin will deign to give me just and propitious words!

All men are naturally vain. There is, however, a pride that is more subtle, more dangerous, and more difficult to cure than any other, that of pious souls. In the Temple, Mary did not cling complacently to the favors she received. Some devout persons lose considerable time scrutinizing their progress in virtue. If they experience some sweetness or consolation in prayer, they become ecstatic and immediately see themselves as favored by God. Yet, these insignificant feelings often come from purely natural sources.

In the Temple, Mary preferred herself to no one. Certain pious souls judge their neighbor with extreme severity. It is not that they occasionally let loose biting remarks about the exterior faults of others. Indeed, their conscience forbids them to utter such caustic remarks—regrettable without doubt—but which are not in themselves grave sins. They do not do this, but instead very candidly and sincerely think themselves superior to those who do not cast sighing looks of longing towards the Blessed Sacrament.

In the Temple, Mary had no suspicion of the sublime mission God had reserved for her. Occasionally one finds pious souls who think they have some special mission. They apply themselves to a thousand devotional practices that God has not asked of them but neglect the most essential aspects of their state in life. The seventeenth century produced one of these false saints who believed herself called to finally make "pure love" known to the world. She unabashedly described herself as the most perfect image of the spouse from the Canticle of Canticles. For a while, she led astray even the enlightened mind of Fenelon[15] by her dangerous delusions.

Let us sincerely examine our consciences. If we find some complacency or fail to consider our complete nothingness, then we are undoubtedly dragging along miserably at the basest level of mediocrity. God cannot pour His gifts into a proud heart. When He discovers a soul that is full of itself, either He lets it stagnate or He uses the only means of healing it, allowing it to fall prey to its own faults—at times considerable—in order for it to open its eyes and recognize its miserable state.

In fact, Saint Peter preferred himself to the other apostles when he said: "Although all may abandon Thee, I will never leave Thee.... Even though I should die with Thee..." In vain the Master reminds him of his weakness, but Peter stubbornly replies, "I will not deny you."[16] Poor Saint Peter! How harshly he learned the lesson so necessary to humility.

If you seriously want to progress in the way of perfection, beg the Queen of Heaven to inspire you with true humility. Never think yourself better than others. Recall the words of Our Lord Himself to the Pharisees, so self-righteous with their exterior acts of justice. I would not dare refer to such words had the Master not pronounced them Himself. "There are sinful souls whom you despise," He declared to these proud men. "But because they recognize the depth of their depravity, My grace will one day touch them. They will enter the Kingdom of Heaven before you."[17]

* * *

I would like to have continued studying the other excellent virtues Mary practiced during her childhood. I would like to have shown Our Lady waiting with impatience for the coming of the Messiah. She knew that the time fixed by the Prophets approached. She meditated with particular fervor on the chapter of Scripture wherein Isaiah foretells the humiliation and suffering of the Man-God. She ardently asked Our Heavenly Father for the particular favor of serving the Lord. Her prayers were granted far beyond her expectations.

I would also like to have studied the vow by which she consecrated her virginity to the Lord. Through such a radiant example, we would have learned how the Most High crowns Christian virginity with admirable fecundity. To develop these topics would exceed the confines of the present work. We have chosen the virtues of the Immaculate Virgin that we deemed most appropriate for souls desiring to lead a profound interior life.

* * *

When speaking of the Savior's childhood at Nazareth, the Gospel tells us that He grew in age, wisdom, and grace before both God and men. Our Lady's childhood, like that of her Divine Son, was also a time of growth. The Virgin quickly rose to peaks of holiness.

During the years she lived in the Temple, she blossomed fully in physical beauty and especially in the radiant splendor of her incomparable virtue. She was now ready for the great designs of the Lord's divine mercy. The luminous radiance of divine maternity would soon engulf her.

Let us ask the holy Virgin to be not only our model but, even more, our guide along the way of perfection. Under her guidance, we will have neither illusions nor dangers to fear, as Saint Bernard assures us.[18] She will lead us on the surest and most direct route to God.

CHAPTER V
The Annunciation

Out of love for us, the Eternal Word was made flesh in the chaste womb of Mary. His plan was marvelously arranged. From all eternity, He chose a man after His heart who would be the virginal spouse of His divine Mother, His adopted father on earth, and the guardian of His childhood. While not granting Joseph the same privileges He had granted our Blessed Mother, the Lord adorned his soul with the rarest virtues and raised him to great holiness.

When Our Lady had completed her education in the Temple, she was wed to this humble artisan. Like her, Saint Joseph belonged to the royal race of David, then fallen from its ancient splendor. Also like her, he had consecrated his virginity to God and ardently desired to see with his own eyes the promised Messiah, the salvation of Israel.

The Most High had prepared this excellent union by revealing His will to these humble and obedient souls. Mary accepted Joseph as the guarantor of Divine Providence, while Joseph received Mary as a precious treasure entrusted to him by Heaven. Neither one nor the other suspected what blessings the Lord would lavish on their modest dwelling. The young spouses had lived but a short time in the little house of Nazareth when the scene of the Annunciation took place in all of its divine simplicity.

* * *

The last days of March had brought the return of spring to the Galilean countryside. The fig trees had begun to unfold their ample leaves and the doves to build their nests in the hollows of the rocks. Flowers dotted the rejuvenated fields. Soon another flower, infinitely more precious, would blossom from the root of Jesse.

In Heaven, the Holy Ghost acclaimed the spotless conception of the Immaculate Virgin with admiration and seemed impatient for the hour when the work of His infinite charity would be fulfilled. No longer did the Divine Spouse wish to delay. He resolved to send an extraordinary messenger to her whom He called "My Spouse"—*Soror mea, sponsa*.[19]

God chose the Archangel Gabriel from among the princes of the celestial court who remained constantly before the throne of the Almighty. He entrusted to him the most important and glorious assignment ever confided to a creature, the mission of announcing to the Virgin the awesome mystery of the Incarnation.

All Heaven now looked upon that simple house of Nazareth, where a profound peace reigned. Joseph probably rested from his hard labor. In the adjoining room, his virgin spouse was praying. The angel appeared and respectfully bowed before his Queen. His countenance resplendent with supernatural joy, he said to her, "Hail, Mary, full of grace, the Lord is with thee."[20]

Saint Gabriel uttered but the strictest truth. At the moment of Mary's conception, divine grace flooded her magnificent soul. Ever since then, this grace had grown ceaselessly in proportions far surpassing our feeble understanding. Now, at this moment, the adorable Trinity wanted this already extraordinary holiness to shine with even greater brilliance: Our Lady would shelter in her womb the

THE ANNUNCIATION

very Author of grace.

Yet, the Archangel's salutation troubled the Immaculate Virgin. By divine enlightenment she had long understood the immensity of God and the nothingness of creatures. In her prodigious humility, she considered herself the lowliest of creatures and thus wondered at receiving such praise. She pondered what hidden meaning could be shrouded in such words.

Seeing this most incomparably perfect of all creatures with such a humble opinion of herself, the celestial ambassador exulted with admiration. "Mary," he said to the trembling Virgin, "fear not, for thou hast found grace with God."[21]

Marriage of the Virgin Mary to Saint Joseph. Fresco in the Basilica of Our Lady of Good Counsel, Genazzano, Italy.

Then slowly, majestically, in the name of the Eternal God, he communicated his sublime message: "Behold, thou shalt conceive in thy womb and shalt bring forth a son, and thou shalt call His name Jesus. He shall be great and shall be called the Son of the Most High, and the Lord God shall give unto Him the throne of David His father, and He shall reign in the house of Jacob forever, and of His kingdom there shall be no end."[22]

These words were far too clear to Our Lady for any hesitation in grasping them. She immediately understood the incomparable honor reserved for her. It seems that she experienced no hesitation on account of her virginity. Indeed, it would be a gratuitous insult to her intelligence to suspect her of such ignorance. She was aware of the prophecy of Isaiah that the Emmanuel would be born of a virgin. Rather, she simply sought to know how God, so rich in miracles, would accomplish such a marvel. "How shall this be done," she asked the angel, "for I know not man?"[23]

"The Holy Ghost shall come upon thee, and the power of the Most High shall overshadow thee. Therefore, the child which shall be born of thee shall be called holy, the Son of God. And behold, thy cousin Elizabeth, she also hath conceived a son in her old age; and this is the sixth month with her who is called barren; for nothing shall be impossible with God."[24]

Profound silence filled that small room in Nazareth, one of those dramatic silences wherein the world's destiny hangs in the balance. The angel had ceased speaking and Mary was quiet.

How many thoughts crowded in upon her! In her mind's eye, she saw the resplendent crown divine motherhood would place on her head, yet she remained too profoundly humble for any complacency about this singular grandeur. She saw the indescribable joys that would surely fill her heart when holding her dear treasure against her bosom, her Jesus, both God and infant. Yet again, her self-mortification would not allow that she be guided by the allure of joy alone, even the most holy of joys.

She also saw the awful martyrdom that would rend her soul. Through Holy Scripture she knew that the Messiah would be delivered to His death like a tender lamb to the slaughter. She foresaw and heard the mournful cry: "I am a worm, and no man; the reproach of men, and the outcast of the people."[25] Yet, such was her fortitude that she would not allow future sorrow to dishearten her.

Above everything, she saw the extremely lofty, fatherly, and holy will of God. She owed obedience to Him; she did not hesitate.

The Immaculate Virgin at last broke the solemn silence. The angel waited to receive her consent in the name of the Holy Ghost. In accepting, she pronounced one of those sublime expressions that only the genius of humility can find. It was the most simple and modest formula of a soul completely submissive to the will of God: "Behold the handmaid of the Lord; be it done unto me according to thy word."[26]

At that, the grandest of all miracles took place. From the very flesh of the Immaculate Virgin, the Holy Ghost formed a small human body. To this body He joined a human soul; to this body and soul He united the Second Person of the Most Holy Trinity, the Word of God.

Although it is necessary to explain these three facts separately to make clear what took place, the three took place completely simultaneously as a single act. Not even for a second were this small body and soul separated from the Word.

From that first instant the Child formed in the womb of Our Lady was the Word Incarnate. Without losing her virginity, Mary became the Mother of God, and in becoming the Mother of Christ, our Head, she also became the Mother of men—our Mother.

In this chapter I have simply followed the Gospel narrative step by step. We will later study the nearly infinite dignity the Immaculate Virgin confers on divine motherhood. We shall see how this privilege should inspire our Christian hearts to great respect, deep gratitude, limitless confidence, and filial devotion. But let us first complete our meditation on this mystery.

Through God's infinite love for us, the Word utterly humbled Himself in the womb of the Virgin. At the same time, other events took place in her soul. When God entrusts a mission to one of His creatures, He also provides the grace to accomplish it fully. Thus, the Most High, having granted a double motherhood to the Blessed Virgin Mary (to be mother of God and of men), conferred upon her a love that was doubly maternal. Such was the splendor in this work of grace that we will never perfectly understand it. Never will we completely understand the ardor of Mary's love for Jesus or the merciful goodness by which the Virgin loves each one of us in particular. Indeed, were we to further reflect upon this mystery, we would pray to her with greater fervor, and serve her with greater zeal. She, in turn, would lavish torrents of grace on us.

The Incarnation had just been completed. Our Lady remained in ecstasy. Every theologian agrees that during this thrice-holy moment God raised her to the most sublime contemplation a pure creature can attain upon earth. Perhaps she was even granted a momentary glimpse of the beatific vision.

The Archangel Gabriel had fulfilled his mission. Upon his arrival he had respectfully bowed before the Queen of heaven. Before departing, he prostrated himself, for Mary was no longer alone. In true justice, the Child she bore in her womb merited the adoration of the archangel, who adored the God-made-man and then returned to Heaven.

* * *

From this mystery, we must draw a stronger and deeper devotion to the Blessed Virgin. The Church, which encourages us to pay special honor to the Immaculate Mother, does not wish to place her on the same level as the Most High. While Mary reigns over all the angels and saints in Heaven, she is still but a simple creature and, accordingly, an infinite distance stands between her and her adorable Son.

Nevertheless, God has united Jesus and Mary so intimately that we cannot separate Them. By consenting to the work of the eternal God, Our Lady has become *ipso facto* the moral cause of our salvation. She is morally necessary for us to go to Jesus.

Souls today are powerfully attracted to the Heart of Jesus. To penetrate this adorable Heart, the sanctuary of the Divinity, more fully, we must go through Mary. Let us ask Our Lady for the sovereign grace of placing us confidently in the arms of Jesus and there, upon His heart, let us rest both in time and in eternity.

CHAPTER VI
The Divine Motherhood

The Gospels, which carefully recount the life of our Savior, provide few details on the Blessed Virgin. They tell us nothing of her spotless conception, nothing of her nativity, and nothing of her childhood in the Temple of Jerusalem. Although the Evangelists develop at length the admirable scenes of the Annunciation and the Visitation, these are the only two mysteries in which Mary appears as a central figure. Subsequently, we find only extremely brief allusions in the Gospel as to her role. We see her presenting her newborn Son to be adored by the poor shepherds and the three kings. Then we see her bearing the Child Jesus to Egypt in hurried flight. Passing references alone indicate her long life of intimacy with the divine Master in the little house of Nazareth.

When Our Lord finally begins his public ministry, the figure of Mary almost disappears into discreet shadows. We see her only for a moment at the wedding in Cana. Here and there the sacred writers mention her humbly listening to her Son teaching the crowds. We find her at last on Calvary, standing at the foot of the cross during the tragic hours of the Passion. That is all the Gospels tell us of Mary. Does it not seem that our piety would gain much from knowing more about so moving a subject?

The Fathers of the Church asked themselves the reason for this strange silence. They unanimously responded that, in establishing the Savior's genealogy, Saint Matthew sums up Our Lady's greatness and glory in a single line. "Jacob," he writes, "begot Joseph, the husband of Mary, of whom was born Jesus, who is called Christ."[27]

Thus, if you desire a more profound knowledge of Mary's role, study with pious attention the most incomparable of her privileges, her divine motherhood.

* * *

I will not conceal from you the almost insurmountable difficulties presented by such a sublime topic. Before broaching the subject, I reread several passages from the many discourses devoted to her by the Doctors of the Church. I was not surprised to see that in the presence of such greatness, they felt overwhelmed by great discouragement. What words would be strong enough to convey their thoughts? What comparisons true enough to communicate such a mystery?

Saint Epiphanius, one of the most brilliant of the Eastern Church Fathers, recounts one by one all the glories of Heaven. He examines the choirs of angels and the different categories of saints. He then adds: "But the Mother of the Word far surpasses them all. Save for God, she is superior to all. No human tongue can worthily sing her praises."[28]

Our Lady Star of the Sea. Statue in the Church of Saint Sylvester, Rome.

Saint Thomas Aquinas, the uncontested master of Catholic Tradition, tells us that divine Maternity confers an infinite dignity upon Mary. He shows us Our Lady reaching the boundaries of the divinity in her ascent to God.[29]

An abyss separates us from the Most High. While we are nothing, He lives in all eternity in light inaccessible to our mortal eyes. Though we can do nothing of ourselves, He created the universe by the power of a single word. Deserving our adoration, He reminds us that our homage serves Him no purpose. "To what purpose do you offer Me the multitude of your victims? saith the Lord. I am full; I desire not holocausts or rams, and fat of fatlings, and blood of calves, and lambs, and goats."[30]

Nevertheless, while this God is sovereignly independent from His creatures, He chose to have recourse to the Immaculate Virgin to accomplish the great designs of His Infinite Mercy. To solicit her consent in the work of the Incarnation, He sent the Archangel Gabriel.

This God, so distant from our smallness, chose to establish such a profound relationship with Mary that I dare say she enters, as no other, into the very intimacy of the adorable Trinity.

The Holy Ghost miraculously fructified her incomparable virginity, becoming her Spouse. Secondly, the Eternal Word drew from her flesh His most holy body and infinitely precious blood. After His birth in the grotto of Bethlehem, He was nourished for many months by Our Lady. This truth so charms and delights us that we exclaim with Saint Augustine, "The flesh of Christ is the flesh of Mary!"—*Car Christi, car Mariae.* Since children's traits are often similar to those of their mothers, the Savior, the most beautiful of children, most probably wanted to resemble Mary.

THE DIVINE MOTHERHOOD

Finally, the Queen of Heaven shares in the Father's glory. He, Who eternally begets the Son, says to Him at the moment of His baptism: "Thou art My beloved Son; in Thee I am well pleased."[31] Mary did not give Our Lord His divine nature, but clothed His divinity with a mortal body similar to our own. Together with the Father, she can say of Jesus, the immortal King of ages, the Word that fills the blessed in Heaven with awe: "Thou art truly my Son. I gave Thee Thy human life and surrounded Thee with the entire strength of my tenderness, O Beloved of my heart."

By her divine Motherhood, the Blessed Virgin possesses indisputable rights over the Savior.

In the first place, she has rights over His will. The Child Jesus had to obey His mother. The Evangelists clearly call this to our attention by showing Him submissive to both His mother and adopted father: "And He went down with them...and was subject to them."[32]

Nevertheless, we must not exaggerate this fact. The Savior received from the Most High a mission beyond the authority of Our Lady. Indeed, at the age of twelve He remained in the Temple among the doctors without informing His parents. In so doing, He wanted us to fully understand that while His mother could not command Him in all things, she had a great influence over His adorable will. Was it not also at her request that He worked His first miracle at Cana?

The Blessed Virgin also has rights over the heart of her Son, and these are inalienable. On earth as in Heaven, Jesus pays His mother the entire respect and tenderness of a son. It is therefore impossible that He would refuse to fulfill her wishes. It is likewise impossible that He would reject our prayers if we present them in the name of the love which is and always will be due His mother.

* * *

What should we conclude about this privilege that elevates the Blessed Virgin so high above all other creatures? First of all, it should inspire us with gratitude. We live amid an abundance of supernatural blessings that souls did not possess in ancient times. Right after our births, we were taken to church, where the sacred water of Baptism made us children of God. When the weight of our sins burdens our conscience too heavily, we relieve the burden of our scruples and remorse at the foot of the altar. We depart with lightened souls and the certitude of having received pardon. When tempted, we can seek strength or consolation amid our labors by kneeling in prayer before the altar. Jesus is truly present, waiting to open His heart to us. In the Tabernacle

Our Lady of the Blessed Sacrament. Church of Saint Claudius, Rome.

He anxiously awaits the offer of the hospitality of our fragile and wretched souls. These graces, running in unceasing torrents upon the world, are at our disposition. We need only take a step to be engulfed by them.

Have you ever supposed you might somehow be indebted to the divine motherhood of the Virgin Mary? Have you ever thought to express your gratitude to her? One day Our Lord cured ten lepers. These miraculously healed and blessed men immediately presented themselves to the priests as prescribed by the Mosaic Law. Only one returned to thank his Benefactor. "Were not ten made clean? Where are the nine?" asked the Savior sadly.[33] Could not the Blessed Virgin say the same? "I gave Jesus to souls and they forget that they received Him through me."

Therefore, let us thank Our Lady today. Indeed, let us thank her often for what she has done for us! This simple practice will call down upon us abundant blessings.

Once again, divine motherhood should inspire us to unlimited confidence. Mary is all good and her prayers are "all-powerful" with God. Let us frequently invoke her.

When Saint John the Apostle reached a very old age he would have his disciples carry him among the faithful whose pastor he was. He often addressed them with the same words: "My children," he pleaded, "love one another." His listeners eventually grew weary of hearing the same teaching and asked him: "Why do you always repeat these same words?" The beloved disciple, who had learned charity from the bosom of the Savior, responded: "to love one another is the Master's command."

If you are surprised that I should insist in telling you to pray without ceasing to your Mother in Heaven, I shall answer: "It is the great means of perseverance and salvation."

God entrusted to us this precious key which opens the Heart of Jesus, the richest of all treasures. We would be remiss in not drawing from it the abundant consolation, illumination, and strength we need for the journey.

We hear much talk about efficacious prayers. There are very efficacious prayers to Saint Expeditus, for example. There are efficacious novenas to other saints who, with the Church, I profoundly venerate. Yet, there is one saint who far surpasses the other elect in glory and power. There is one prayer that is the most perfect of all after the one taught us by Our Lord Himself.

With this prayer and with the humility that is so pleasing to God, we ask for the necessary graces for the present moment as well as for our final hour. "Pray for us sinners now and at the hour of our death." The whole prayer is really quite ingenious, for it includes the Blessed Virgin's magnificent privileges—her Immaculate Conception and her sublime motherhood. It also contains within it an act of praise addressed to the divine Son she so dearly loves: "And blessed is the fruit of thy womb, Jesus." Our Lady cannot help but hear this prayer and be moved!

Saint Bernard habitually greeted a statue of the Madonna in his monastery. Each time he passed by he recited a Hail Mary. A legend says that one day the statue came to life and Our Lady's face lit up with a smile. She graciously inclined her head to the saint and said, "And I greet you, Bernard."

Let us be devoted to the Hail Mary. Let us often recite it with attention and piety. The Blessed Virgin may not miraculously greet us as she did Saint Bernard, but she will protect us during our lifetime. She will come to our aid at the hour of our need with maternal love and will lead our souls

to the Paradise of which she is the Queen.

CHAPTER VII
The Visitation

After the salutation of the Archangel Gabriel, the Incarnate Word was conceived in the womb of the Blessed Virgin Mary. In the prayerful silence that enshrouded the humble dwelling when the angel departed, Mary gradually emerged from her ecstasy. With the delightful simplicity which gives her perfect beauty such a poignant charm, she returned to the routine of ordinary life. She told no one—not even Saint Joseph—about the marvels the Holy Ghost had worked within her.

Having learned of the expectant hope of her cousin Elizabeth, Mary felt a strong desire to visit her. In the opinion of most approved commentators, she spent a few more days in Nazareth before departing.

March was drawing to a close and the solemn feast of Passover was quickly approaching. She probably waited until the holy days in order to travel to Jerusalem with Saint Joseph. When they had fulfilled their religious duties, Mary set off for the city of Hebron where Zachary lived. It seems improbable that Saint Joseph accompanied her in this second part of the journey. If he had, he would not have been ignorant several months later regarding the divine secret of his holy spouse.

Meanwhile, the Immaculate Virgin arrived at her cousin's house where the Visitation, faithfully recorded by Saint Luke, took place. This mystery, so valuable for our piety, helps us understand Our Lady's virtues and her role in the sanctification of our souls.

The Evangelist shows Mary hurriedly climbing the mountain road toward Hebron. "And Mary, rising up in those days, went into the hill country with haste into a city of Juda. And she entered into the house of Zachary and saluted Elizabeth."[34] Why did she so joyfully hasten to Juda? Was she moved by the desire to share her radiant secret with Elizabeth as soon as possible, as though her soul were too tender to bear alone the overwhelming significance of such bliss? Did she hope to pour out her heart entirely to her cousin, whose perfect goodwill she had esteemed for so long a time? Certainly this thought did not occur to the silent Virgin who always displayed great discretion. In fact, when arriving at Zachary's house, she did not initiate the exchange of secrets. Heavenly inspiration first prompted Elizabeth, the mother of the Precursor, to speak so that Mary would allow the emotion flooding her soul to overflow into divine song.

Reasons of a higher order had moved the Virgin to undertake this journey. Elizabeth and her husband enjoyed a higher social status. They were highly regarded in the region, and Providence had abundantly blessed them with the fruits of the earth. In their prosperity they had not forgotten their poorer relatives, Saint Joachim and Saint Anne, who had done many favors for them. Many years earlier Zachary's influence had undoubtedly contributed greatly to Mary's admission among the children raised in the Temple at Jerusalem. Hence, the fair-hearted Virgin wished to manifest her affectionate gratitude to her generous relatives. She wanted to pay Elizabeth the kindest and tenderest attention, for she to whom God had miraculously granted a child was already advanced in age and had been barren for many years. The Virgin's ever-

THE VISITATION

The Visitation by Carl Bloch.

attentive charity made her joyfully sacrifice her own rest and divine consolation. Would it not have been better, however, for Our Lady to remain quietly within her peaceful retreat, her small room in Nazareth, glowing still with the memory of the Annunciation? Would she not have found there more sweetness in praying to the Incarnate Word, really present within her? Certainly, but she did not think selfishly of herself.

When Jesus enters a heart, He inspires it with love of neighbor. "A new commandment I give unto you: That you love one another," He said at the Last Supper, "as I have loved you. By this shall all men know that you are my disciples, if you have love one for another. Greater love than this no man hath, that a man lay down his life for his friends."[35]

The lessons of this mystery are legion. We must be attentive to the needs of those around us and share generously with the poor. Our souls must be moved at the sight of the suffering who cry out to us. We must let blossom the goodness planted in our hearts by our Heavenly Father, the divine flower of the Christian life. Our hearts must not harden. If we do not follow these lessons, we should tremble before the Almighty! We are not the disciples of Him who gave His blood to the last drop, nor will the charitable Virgin of the Visitation regard us as her children!

At last, then, Mary reached her destination. Consider the meeting of these two women: one wealthy, yet the spouse of a merely mortal man; the other undoubtedly poor, yet the Spouse of the Holy Ghost and the Mother of God.

What does the Immaculate Virgin do when she reaches her cousin Elizabeth's home? We are already familiar with the incredible humility of her youth. At the Temple, she considered herself the lowliest of all. Events have now changed entirely! Our Lady carries the eternal Son of the Father within her. She is not oblivious to the great honor such sublime motherhood confers on her. Conscious of her glory, does Mary expect to see her cousin render her honors upon her arrival? Certainly not! Rather, she rushes forward to greet her cousin. With modest grace and delightful spontaneity, she bows before her cousin, embracing her with effusive and tenderest respect.

Elizabeth, however, is inspired by God and greets her cousin by prostrating before her and crying out in admiration: "And whence is this to me, that the mother of my Lord should come to me?"[36] Mary can no longer conceal her secret, already revealed by Heaven. She bursts forth in her admirable canticle of acknowledgment, her *Magnificat*: "My soul doth magnify the Lord; and my spirit hath rejoiced in God my Savior. Because He hath regarded the humility of His handmaid, for behold from henceforth all generations shall call me blessed. He that is mighty hath done great things for me, and holy is His name. And His mercy is from generation unto generation to them that fear Him. He hath showed might in His arm, He hath scattered the proud in the conceit of their heart."[37] Indeed, the more she glorifies the Most High, the more deeply does she engulf herself in the abyss of her nothingness.

This is an important lesson: God grants us favors in the measure that we humble ourselves in His presence. The Holy Ghost does not deposit His gifts in hearts full of self-love.

* * *

The visit of the Blessed Virgin caused an abundance of graces to descend upon the blessed home of Elizabeth and Zachary. In first place, the prophecy of the angel was fulfilled. Saint Gabriel had appeared to Zachary as he offered incense in the Holy of Holies, announcing the birth of John the Baptist and adding that the child would be sanctified while still in his mother's womb! In fact, Mary had only to embrace her cousin Elizabeth for the presence of the Lord within her to purify the soul of His precursor.

Our Lady's role consists in distributing the graces merited by the precious blood of her divine Son. She refuses them to none, for the Savior died on the Cross for all men. But she grants them with greater abundance to the souls who love her with special filial tenderness.

Perhaps you sense the fragility of our wretched human nature. Perhaps, despite your sincere desire to serve God, you commit serious sins. Do not become disheartened in such painful moments; direct your profound cry of distress to Mary and appeal for her help. Pray to her with all your faith and fervor. She will obtain for you the strength to lead a pure life. If a habitual sinner who seems to have one foot in Hell would but beg the Blessed Virgin with perseverance to lift him from his miserable state, his prayer would surely be granted.

Mary's visit to Elizabeth, then, brought lights from on high, so that Elizabeth knew through revelation the mystery of the Incarnation.

You learned your catechism. You know Our Lord. Yet this supernatural understanding has such little influence over your life! Perhaps it even leaves you indifferent and cold! Beg the Immaculate Virgin to help you better understand Christ's abundant love for us. In His infinite tenderness, Our Lord never stops thinking of you, waiting for you at all hours of the day and night in His tabernacle. His adorable heart loved you to the utmost folly of the Cross, and is burning with infinite charity for you. He ardently desires to fill you with His most precious gifts. Jesus wishes you to approach Him with trust— complete trust. Ask Our Lady for the grace to know the Savior better. Indeed, her special mission is to lead souls to Jesus.

Finally, the visit of Mary brought treasures of joy. "For behold, as soon as the voice of thy salutation sounded in my ears, the infant in my womb leaped for joy."[38] God created us for eternal bliss. That is why we carry an unquenchable thirst for happiness within us. Alas! Many think they have found happiness in forbidden pleasures. How far they have strayed! Sin bears the fruit of death, leaving only remorse and disgust in its wake.

Others seek legitimate, but purely human, satisfaction outside Our Lord. Human love can distract us for a moment, but in the end it makes us suffer because it cannot satisfy the void in our souls. True joy is found in hearts that give themselves entirely to Christ.

O Immaculate Virgin, Mother of holy joy, grant our souls, thirsting for happiness, the indescribable joys of Divine Love.

CHAPTER VIII
Mary's Sanctification

When Solomon wanted to raise a temple for the Lord on Mount Moriah, it took him seven full years to build. He called upon the talents of the East's most prominent artisans and erected a masterpiece of beauty and magnificence. Large open spaces paved with stone slabs surrounded the holy edifice. The Levites maintained a perpetual fire on the bronze altar, a touching symbol of the Divine charity unceasingly burning for love of us without ever exhausting the resources of His infinite tenderness. The priests sacrificed the victims offered to the Most High on this altar while the faithful attended the religious ceremonies at a distance.

Extraordinary richness adorned Yahweh's house. The inside walls disappeared entirely under the cypress wainscoting encrusted with precious metals. Golden seven-branched candelabras surrounded the ten golden tables where the loaves of proposition were placed. Behind the purple veil concealing the Holy of Holies, two Cherubim, made of the finest gold, sheltered the Ark of the Covenant, the glory of Israel, with outstretched wings. Once a year, the high priest entered this awe-inspiring sanctuary where the chosen people of God kept the Tables of the Law and a few fragments of manna.

God had resolved to build another temple whose dignity would far surpass that of His ancient dwelling. From this temple, the Eternal Word would take on flesh like our own and form the body He would immolate on the Cross and give to us as food in the Eucharist. From this living temple, the Most High fashioned the greatest of His marvels, thus elevating the Immaculate Virgin to incomparable perfection.

In this chapter, we will study Mary's sanctification. Although we will never fully understand this sublime work of grace, we will find lessons helpful for our salvation by meditating upon this work of God.

* * *

Theologians distinguish two consecutive stages in the sanctification of Our Lady. The first took place at the moment of her spotless conception. Mary's soul emerged from the Creator's hand all innocent and pure, and endowed with the rarest of virtues. From that moment, the Virgin, resplendent with supernatural beauty, surpassed in holiness not only the most glorious angel, but all the angels and saints together. Thus did the Holy Ghost deposit this first jewel in the crown of His future Spouse.

The admirable treasures of this first "dowry" produced abundant fruit. Nothing is simpler than our heavenly Mother's singular correspondence with grace, yet nothing is more inspiring for our piety.

She seeks nothing extraordinary for ascending from virtue to virtue, nor is she ambitious for the exceptional missions that Providence sometimes entrusts to souls. Indeed, before the angel's salutation, she did not even suspect that she was the Virgin chosen from all eternity. She does not expect heroic sacrifices whereby she would shed her blood in profusion. Instead, she completely surrenders her future to the Heavenly Father.

Her interior life can be entirely summed up as a double movement of great simplicity and prodigious strength. She hastened, threw, and veritably engulfed herself in the abyss of her own nothingness, then soared to God with equal vigor in the fullness of her humility and love.

Every one of her actions, even the most ordinary, is perfumed with the aroma of deliberate humility and abundant charity. Not for a second in all her lifetime did she remove her eyes from the Infinite Beauty, nor ever fail to remain lowly. Even while sleeping she remained virtuous, for she did this also with an obedient heart. She can truthfully say, then, with the spouse of the Canticle of Canticles: "I sleep, and my heart watcheth."[39]

What is the result of such constant interior life? Mary's soul grows in holiness at an ever-increasing rate. Her love expands with an ever-more-blazing ardor like the windswept fires in forests desiccated by summer's heat. So many are her accumulated merits that we abstain from calculating them even from afar.

Do not think such progress in virtue was easy for the Blessed Virgin! She certainly experienced no inner temptations, since her Immaculate Conception sheltered her from concupiscence. Just like her divine Son, however, she was subject to the law of effort.

Jesus endured and was often overwhelmed by fatigue. The Gospel narrative shows Jesus exhausted and sleeping in a boat while the tempest rages and huge waves lash the bow. We see Him, yet again, forced by weariness to sit on the edge of Jacob's well. Since Mary was not given more privileges than Our Lord, we can be certain she did not reach her incomparable holiness without effort.

God did not preserve us from original sin as He did the

Mother of the Incarnate Word. Yet, on the day of our baptism, He erased its trace from our souls. When, having had the misfortune of offending Him, we repent, He forgives our sins and, through the sacrament of Penance, we are reconciled to Him. Like Mary, we, too, must make these gifts from Heaven fruitful.

If you want to progress in the interior life, imitate the double action we have admired and observed in the heart of Our Lady. Begin by humbling yourself. Should God allow you to fall into grave sin, make use of this humiliation. Do not forget your wretchedness, having fully experienced its weight. Should the Heavenly Father have preserved you from mortal sin, all the more reason to be humble. Saint Francis Borgia deemed himself beneath Satan. Indeed, he thought himself capable, without the help of grace, of any crime!

Finally, carry out your duties in life faithfully, because such is the adorable will of God. This, briefly, is the secret of holiness. Should you stray from this path, you will find only dangers and illusions!

* * *

The second sanctification of Mary lasted nine months, from the Annunciation to the birth of Our Lord in the manger at Bethlehem. His intimate and prolonged union with His mother worked miracles of grace in her that were more indescribable than the previous ones! How could it have been otherwise?

We know from the Gospels that Our Lord's presence has a sovereign efficacy. A supernatural virtue emanated from His person which both healed the sick and transformed hearts. "And all the multitude sought to touch Him, for

power went out from Him and healed all."[40]

A poor woman who had been sick for many years said to herself: "If I shall touch only His garment, I shall be healed."[41] Carefully she slipped through the crowd surrounding Jesus. When she finally reached Him, she silently and discreetly touched the hem of His cloak with her hand. She was immediately healed.

The sinner Mary Magdalene prostrated herself at the Savior's feet, covering them with her kisses and bathing them with her tears. Through this divine contact, the flood of her iniquities was overwhelmed by the even greater flood of His divine mercy.

Yet, the power of Our Lord's presence did not affect everyone equally. Many who knew Him on this earth did not allow grace to touch their hardened hearts, nor did they recognize the Master. They were devoid of faith. The healing power of Our Lord's divine presence acted upon others according to the degree of their faith.

How completely did Our Lord's presence affect the soul of Our Lady! Her beautiful conscience presented no obstacle to the work of His mysterious action. Indeed, the heart of the Virgin remained pure and spotless. Her faith was unfailing, her confidence unshakable, and her love seemed boundless. During the nine months of her pregnancy an ocean of grace flooded her.

To work the salvation of your soul, Jesus wishes to enter your heart. In the Holy Eucharist, He communicates His infinite life to increase the action of sanctifying grace within you. He thus causes His rays to shine in your heart, allowing supernatural virtues to blossom. He brings you His precious blood so that this beneficial dew quench the fire of concupiscence in your body. The Eucharist is the bread of angels and the wine that engenders virgins.

The Real Presence of the Savior in this sacrament is just as efficacious as His visible presence on earth. Jesus lost none of His power or love by ascending into Heaven. Why then do you draw such scant fruit from your Communions? It is because you present obstacles to His divine action!

The Presentation by Diaz Tavares.

"What obstacles?" you might ask. You are too faithful to receive Holy Communion poorly disposed. Likewise, it is not sin which prevents the sacramental action of divine grace from taking place in you. No, the obstacle is a lack of trust. You simply do not sufficiently esteem the indescribable visit of the Body and Blood of Our Savior. You do not pray to Our Lord with the burning faith and holy expectation that conquers Our Lord's heart. In those precious moments of actual grace, present to Him the litany of your woes. Mention them all without forgetting a single one. Say to Him: "I believe firmly that from this heap of dung Thou canst cause virtues to flourish. I ask Thee this in the name of Thy promises, and I go as far as to demand that Thou dost transform my heart. Day and night will I cry out to Thee until Thou dost accomplish this miracle of love."

Without doubt, He will tell you what He told others during His ministry: "As you have believed, so be it done to thee."[42] If your trust is small, you will obtain little; if it is great, you will obtain much.

* * *

Perhaps your faith is asleep. Perhaps you are gripped by secret anxieties. Ask the Blessed Virgin to inspire you with an unshakable trust in Jesus truly present in the Eucharist. Ask her for this favor in the name of her maternal love and the name of the final words of her agonizing Son to her on the Cross. Whatever your weakness or pain, surrender them with closed eyes to God Who loves you to the point of concealing Himself for you under the veil of the Host.

CHAPTER IX
The Finding of Our Lord in the Temple

When the heartless Herod died, the angel of the Lord immediately informed Joseph that the life of the divine Child was no longer in danger. The Holy Family left Egypt and returned to Galilee. The sight of the houses of Nazareth on the horizon at the end of that long and perilous journey filled Mary, carrying Jesus in her arms, with sweet consolation. Surely she would encounter precious memories upon returning to her humble dwelling.

It was there that she enjoyed thirty years of incredible bliss, watching the tender unfolding of the Incarnate Word. Indeed, Our Lord's human nature developed according to natural law. His unbounded holiness and divine wisdom, on the other hand, could not increase, for infinity, by the very fullness of its perfection, is immutable. Nevertheless, Jesus wanted to reveal the treasures of His eternal wisdom gradually. Mary exultantly observed the progress of her beloved Son and entered more fully each day into His inebriating beauty.

One shadow of sorrow darkened those years of intimate joy. The mysterious sword foretold by Simeon pierced Our Lady's soul and plunged into the intimacy of her heart. Aside from the drama of Calvary, this was the most cruel martyrdom of her entire lifetime: She lost the Child Jesus.

* * *

Mary and Joseph journeyed to Jerusalem each year to celebrate the Passover feast. When the Savior reached the age of twelve, He accompanied His parents to the Holy City. At that age, young Israelites became sons of the law and had to participate in liturgical ceremonies.

The great solemnities took place with their usual splendor, and the hour of departure sounded. The pilgrims of Galilee, separated from their homeland by a three-day journey, casually formed small groups as they walked. The groups, spread out along the road during the journey, would gather again in the evening at an inn where all would spend the night.

The Blessed Virgin and Saint Joseph, although not seeing the Child with them, were not concerned, for both assumed that Jesus accompanied others of their traveling acquaintances. For an entire day they continued their journey tranquilly. When night fell and everyone assembled at the first stop, they were surprised that the Child Jesus did not return to them. Thus, they "sought Him among their kinfolks and acquaintances."[43] Looking throughout the camp and questioning each group, their fears mounted. Jesus was nowhere to be found.

What agony overwhelmed Mary's heart! To understand the depth of her suffering, it is necessary to understand the breadth of her love for this One who was both her Son and her God. She had entirely surrendered her virginal heart to Jesus. He, her joy, her reason for living, her entire life, was gone.

Uncertainty inclined her heart to anguish. She had no doubt that Our Lord was the Word Incarnate, but that did not prevent her from fearing for His life. Had she not seen Him suffer from cold? Had she not seen Him hungry and tired like other children? Perhaps some accident had befallen Him. Had she not seen Him hunted by the murderous rage of men like Herod? Had yet another enemy attempted to harm Him?

How often had she meditated on the Scripture passages in which Isaiah prophesied the suffering of the Messiah! She knew not when and how this noble sacrifice would take place. Had the time of His martyrdom already arrived? An ocean of anguish engulfed her soul.

Our Lady exercised the highest form of virtue during those fearful moments. The holiest of God's creatures, preserved by an exceptional life-long privilege from even the slightest imperfection, examined her conscience. Pious authors say she feared being guilty of some negligence. Imbued with the sense of her lowliness, she thought herself unworthy to care for Our Lord.

To her feelings of unworthiness, Mary joined prayer and action. Nightfall rendered it almost impossible to continue the search, so she spent the entire night imploring the mercy of our Heavenly Father. At daybreak, she and Saint Joseph returned along the same road they had traveled the previous day. Together they walked, grief-stricken, seeking the Child Jesus at every turn, hoping to see Him hastening to return to them.

At times in our spiritual journey, we also lose Jesus. I am not speaking here of sin, which indeed vigorously chases the Divine Friend from our souls. Rather, I speak of the moment when, without our having gravely offended Him, Our Lord removes Himself from our grasp. He seems to flee from us, even to abandon us.

At those moments, we no longer fulfill our duties easily. It is as if grace were withdrawn from us. The joy of our heart diminishes and we no longer feel anything but suffering and self-contempt. Times of temptation become even more difficult and painful. Eternal justice inspires within us a holy fear; doubt, horrible doubt, cripples us. Has God forgiven our sins? Does He, far away in Heaven, even consider our nothingness? Has He any compassion on our misery? What will become of us, so utterly deprived of all help and joy?

In such painful moments, let us imitate Mary and humble ourselves all the more profoundly before God. At these times we must especially continue our prayer despite the aridity or the darkness in which our souls are plunged.

Do you imagine that the Child Jesus had ceased loving Mary in the abyss of her suffering? No, His divine heart observed her with great compassion in her immense distress. Indeed, invisibly present to her, He remained close by, supporting her with His all-powerful grace. Allowing her this suffering, He gave the world a great lesson in detachment and obedience to His holy will.

Even when He seems withdrawn from you, the Good Shepherd does not cease loving you. We have only to let ourselves be led, eyes closed and with profound trust. "For though I should walk in the midst of the shadow of death, I will fear no evils, for thou art with me. Thy rod and thy staff, they have comforted me,"[44] the psalmist sings. Even though I no longer feel Thy presence, Lord, I believe, I know, that Thou art with me.

At the first light of day, then, Mary and Joseph had retraced their steps to Jerusalem, seeking all day for the Divine Child, but to no avail. Darkness came again, and that night was worse than the previous one for Our Savior's parents. Their hopes of finding the Child along the road to the Holy City had been dashed.

On the morning of the third day, Mary and Joseph entered

the Temple. Under the archways, they saw an attentive crowd gathered around the learned men of Israel. There, among the teachers, was Jesus, asking them questions and thoughtfully listening to their responses. Such profound and heavenly wisdom sprang from His lips that the doctors, captivated, questioned Him in turn. Equally astonished were Mary and Joseph. Seeing them, the Child rushed into His mother's arms and tenderly embraced her with charming grace.

It is not without mystery that Our Lord allowed Himself to be found in the Temple. If you desire to live in deeper intimacy with Our Lord, seek Him where He speaks to souls: in meditation and prayer.

The Immaculate Virgin closely embraced the Son over Whom she had cried with such anguish and gently whispered tenderly into His ear, "Son, why hast Thou done so to us? Behold, Thy father and I have sought Thee sorrowing."[45]

Let us admire with what tender confidence Mary speaks to her Savior. His greatest servants speak to Him with similar holy familiarity. One particularly trying day, Saint Teresa of Avila said to Our Lord: "If this is how Thou treatest Thy friends, I am hardly surprised Thou hast so few of them!" We should speak to Our Lord with similar ease, laying our troubles and fears before Him. We may even go so far sometimes as to complain to Him—very respectfully, of course, like Saint Teresa—of the great demands of His love for us.

He will respond to you as He did to His mother: "Did you not know that I must be about my Father's business?"[46] He might add: "While hidden, I was accomplishing the work of My mercy in thy soul, showing how insignificant it is without Me and inspiring in it a greater desire for My presence. Blessed are those who hunger and thirst for eternal justice, for they shall be satisfied."

* * *

In a preceding meditation we saw how imprudent it would be to ask God for suffering. Let us humbly accept the trials Providence sends us. When the Master places the heavy burden of the cross on our shoulders, let us cry out to Our Lady of Sorrows to aid us in our troubles. She will restore our serenity. We will see that she is truly the Mother of sweet hope and holy joy.

CHAPTER X
The Blessed Virgin's Compassion

Several days after the birth of her Son, Mary went with Saint Joseph to Jerusalem to present her Newborn to God. Scarcely anyone in the milling crowd within the porticos of the Temple paid any heed to this poor couple. The Incarnate Word had come among His own people, but they knew Him not.

Only Simeon and Anna, moved by heavenly inspiration, had come to adore the Savior. The old man took the Child God into his arms and in the ecstasy of his gratitude he sang his *nunc dimittis:* "Now, Thou dost dismiss Thy servant, O Lord, according to Thy word in peace, because my eyes have seen Thy salvation."[47] Filled with prophetic light, he foresaw moments of great sorrow for Our Lady. Sadly shaking his head, he said to her, "And thy own soul a sword shall pierce."[48]

In Nazareth Our Lady lived in delightful intimacy with her Son for a long time. At last, however, it was necessary for Them to part. Mary often listened attentively to the teachings of her Son during His public ministry. The cries of admiration His supernatural wisdom evoked from the crowds stirred in her motherly heart sweet echoes of the loving exchanges and indescribable daily bliss during Their thirty years together.

Then came the tragic hour the aged Simeon had foreseen in his terrible prophecy. The cross stands out against a

cloud-filled sky that appears to portend eternal punishments. A dreadful silence resounds throughout that city liable for the murder of its God. Jesus is expiring.

At the foot of the gibbet whereon the great Victim is nailed stands Mary, motionless, silent, engulfed in untold grief, and gazing upon the dying God.

What created mind could fully understand her suffering? Such mysteries are unfathomable to our feeble minds. Nevertheless, we will attempt to study the martyrdom of her who is both Mother of the Savior and our Mother.

* * *

Trials afflict us in thousands of ways during our lives. Perhaps they affect us in our material goods. These, surely, can be painful, but they do not touch our persons. "Want of money is not fatal."

We may suffer bodily ills. These are far greater sufferings—our flesh trembles, our sensitivity is overwhelmed. Yet our minds can remain at peace. "A great soul remains master of the body it occupies."

Again, trials may be psychological: doubts, discouragement, jealousy, and despondency cast shadows on life and sometimes render it unbearable. These cause the feeble to languish, to become obsessed, or to lose their minds. But this is not yet the worst sting one may experience in a lifetime.

Trials can strike us in the very depths of our being. Great suffering springs from the heart, caused by wounded love. If no powerful reaction rescues us, the love that had made our dreams come true can take us to our very death.

Mary suffered only through the love she bore her Son, so her martyrdom surpasses in agony the martyrdom of blood.

What was the intensity of her pain? To comprehend it one would have to comprehend the depth of her love. That intensity cannot be compared to our pale sentiments. Our hearts are constricted, while her soul is vast, the masterpiece of God's creation. The selfishness dwelling in our hearts taints even the purest movements of our love. Mary gave herself unreservedly to her Son, for original sin had not tarnished her immaculate heart.

She loved Jesus because He was her son. She bore Him in her womb. She nourished Him and heard His murmured first words. Her soul melted with tenderness when He called her "Mother" for the first time. She witnessed His development through the years. As she watched in awe, the child became a youth with a profound gaze, then a man of riveting divine beauty.

This Son, clothed with every perfection, had given her nothing but the utmost joy. He had revealed to her the treasures of His soul. At her request, He had worked His first miracle. He had given her both His filial love and His obedience.

Mary loved Jesus even more because He was her God. Attaining a certain perfection, love of God is stronger than maternal love. When Saint Jane de Chantal left home to become a religious, her son lay across the threshold to prevent her departure. The poor woman, overcome with grief at this sight, stopped momentarily. Then, with extraordinary courage, she gathered her faltering strength and heroically stepped over the body of her child.

Mary did nothing like this. Her love of God multiplied her motherly love, and this mysterious reckoning produced an almost infinite love.

Now, her so-beloved Son endures before her very eyes the most cruel, the most unjust, the most ignominious of tortures.

She sees Him suffer in His very flesh. Step by step, she follows the somber procession wending its way up to Calvary. She witnesses the horrible scene of the crucifixion, hearing the heavy hammer driving sharp nails into the adorable hands and feet of her Child and seeing the tearing of His flesh and the shedding of His precious blood. When the infamous gibbet is raised between Heaven and Earth, she compassionately follows the course of the agony on the Holy Face.

Mary sees Jesus offended in His honor. He goes to His death in the company of thieves. The henchmen of the high priests mock His goodness, His holiness, His very divinity, while the soldiers jeer: "Let Him now come down from the cross, and we will believe Him."[49]

She sees Him, Whose beatific joys she had known, suffer in the depths of His soul. Immense distress overwhelms her as she hears His cry of agony: "My God, my God, why hast Thou forsaken Me?"[50]

Sacred Scripture says that when Agar, in the desert without resources, saw her son's life ebbing away, she left him under a tree. She then fled and cried out in her despair, "I will not see the boy die."[51] Not for a moment does Mary abandon her agonizing Son, nor does she miss a single moment of His suffering. When Jesus dies, she is at His feet.

Love produces a phenomenon that the medieval philosophers called "ecstasy." They said that love takes the heart, so to speak, of the one who loves and exchanges it with the heart of the beloved. This is how Mary felt. All her Son's sufferings resonated in her. When the soldier's lance pierced the Savior's heart, it simultaneously pierced the Virgin Mother's soul. Simeon's prophecy had come to pass, and she could say with the author of Lamentations: "O all ye that pass by the way, attend and see if there be any sorrow like to my sorrow."[52]

When temptation strikes us, we tremble in our innermost being. We murmur a complaint. We are tempted to accuse God of unfairness while asking ourselves bitterly: "Why am I suffering like this?" When the problem of evil perturbs us so intensely, let us reflect upon the great drama of Calvary.

Did the Father not love His only Son, begotten from all eternity as a luminous hearth generates light? Twice the Father's voice had resounded, at Our Lord's baptism and on Mount Tabor: "This is My beloved Son in Whom I am well pleased."[53]

Did God not love the purest Virgin whom He had made the mother of her Messiah, preserving her from original sin and adorning her with the highest virtues?

Yet, God found no more precious gift for both His Son and His mother than that of suffering.

Through suffering the great work of redemption is accomplished. Through suffering the Master redeemed the world. Through suffering Mary became the sovereign bestower of the grace merited by the blood of Jesus Christ. God sends us suffering to purify and save us. In His merciful goodness, He allows us to use this precious gift not only for our personal good but, even more, for those who are dear to us.

You poor souls who suffer, do not dry your tears. Rather, remember that these tears have great value and can be transformed into a dew of blessing. Do you not have sins to expiate? Do you not have beloved family or friends whose eternal destinies concern you? Do you not perhaps have deceased ones suffering in Purgatory? Accept your sufferings with resignation, gratitude, and love. Present your tears to the agonizing Heart of Jesus. He, from afar, will efficaciously unite you to His work of salvation.

Our Heavenly Father has compassion for our weakness.

He desires that our pain find consolation in its very exacerbation: When suffering reaches a certain intensity, tears flow from our eyes. A crisis ensues, and the awareness of our unhappiness diminishes.

God did not grant this relief to the Queen of Martyrs on Calvary. Without crying, without fainting, without any weakening in body or mind, Mary remained standing at the foot of the cross for the duration of her Son's agony. What power sustained her?

She believed with all her soul in the infinite price of the sacrifice that Divine Justice had awaited for centuries and of which she was also in some way a victim. The Church depicts her looking at the Crucified with sorrowful eyes: "When thou didst gaze on Him with eyes filled with love," sings the Church in the Divine Office, "thou didst contemplate less the horror of His wounds than the triumphant work of Redemption." She saw the future fulfillment of the Savior's words: "When I will be lifted up on the altar of My cross, I will attract the world by the power of My love."[54] To obtain this divine love to enrich and strengthen our lives, she accepted her sorrow with the fullness of her heroic will.

Indeed, closely examine the scene on Golgotha. Agonizing on the cross, Jesus leans towards you, His head crowned with thorns. With blood-filled eyes, from which life is already ebbing, He points to the Virgin shedding the blood of her immaculate heart for you, and with dying voice He says, *"Ecce Mater tua"*—Behold thy mother.[55]

Another thought sustains Mary on Calvary. She was aware of the great plan of Providence: After His humiliation would come His triumph; after His death, the resurrection. Jesus, expiring before her eyes, would once again hold her in His arms in the exultation of victory. Following

Good Friday, she would await Easter, knowing that the Cross would one day be raised as a sign of glorious victory in the sight of men.

At times we curse suffering. Indeed, its hideous face terrifies us. We flee it in horror as one of the mysterious companions of death. Such is the great law that governs the earth: Life is given here below through suffering alone. It is in suffering that we come into the world. It is in suffering that great artists find creative inspiration. It is in suffering that great works are born and come to fruition. Suffering traverses our poor existence as the messenger of joy.

When suffering comes, trust! Gaze toward Heaven filled with hope. Despite the sorrow that besets us, let us know how to patiently await the abundant life it promises us. Suffering perfects our natural qualities. It tempers our character and matures our intelligence. It increases our ability to love and gives our hearts a generosity that can lead to sacrifice.

* * *

May the great lessons the sorrowful Virgin gives us engrave themselves in our minds and transform our lives. When trials befall us, let us no longer doubt, surrender to discouragement, or complain. At the foot of the Cross we have learned the value of suffering. Let us then lovingly receive this gift of God. Let it bear fruit in our lives by our resignation. From its seed will sprout a stem whereon the flower of life will serenely unfold.

At the hour of suffering, let us take courage! We must firmly climb the steep hill of Calvary if we are to one day savor the joys of eternal Easter.

CHAPTER XI
Mary's Death and Assumption

In His gloriously resurrected body, Jesus ascended the Mount of Olives where, a few weeks earlier, He had prayed and sweat blood in agony. He blessed His disciples one last time, then ascended into Heaven by His own power.

A luminous cloud hid Him from the eyes of His Mother and His disciples for some time. Still they tried to penetrate the translucent azure vastness, gazing toward the enchanting eastern sky. The Master's triumph had filled their souls with exultation. A peaceful melancholy blended with their joy, however, for in departing, Christ had taken their hearts.

Two white-robed angels came to recall them to the realities of life. The Virgin and the disciples returned together to the upper room. Mary would spend several more years on earth, where she had savored ineffable joy in intimacy with her Son. His death and resurrection deprived her of His visible presence, but she was to fulfill the role of mother to the budding Church that Our Lord had confided to her.

Separation from her Son weighed heavily on her. Yet she relieved her sadness in daily Communion. Tradition holds that she received the adorable Eucharist from the hands of Saint John the Apostle. With lively faith she encountered, under the appearance of bread, the Body she had formed and nourished, and which she had seen suffer and die for us. Yet she longed to see again face-to-face the Son she so loved.

The longer her exile, the more ardent became her desire. At last, the happy hour sounded when the Master Himself would call her and crown her in Heaven.

* * *

The Immaculate Virgin died.

When carefully reflecting on the privileges of this incomparable queen, we wonder why the Most High made her die. The law condemning guilty humanity to the worst temporal punishments could not bind her who had been conceived without sin. Furthermore, should not this virginal body, having borne Eternal Life for nine months, have drawn radiant immortality from that divine association? These thoughts so vividly impressed Saint Epiphanius that he wrote: "Did Mary really die, or was she but instantaneously transformed into the image of her resurrected Son? This is one of the problems I dare not solve by the light of my own intelligence."[56]

The traditional teaching of the Church leaves us with no doubt on this point. Our Lady truly died.[57]

It is fitting that it should be so. The Savior showed us the way we should follow Him. Mary, the most glorious of pure creatures was not greater than Jesus. It was necessary that, like Him, she render her soul into the hands of the Father and offer Him her last sigh. Our Heavenly Father also willed that by her example she soften our anxiety about this fearful passage.

If the death of the Immaculate was real, it was consoling and peaceful, resembling the quiet falling into sleep of an infant in its crib. It could not have been otherwise. No fear could trouble Mary's radiant conscience. Her soul, all-pure from its first moments, had never been tarnished by the least imperfection. No earthly separation could break her heart: Jesus, her only love, awaited her beyond the tomb. It was her utmost joy to join Him at long last. No suffering tortured her body as she lay dying; she had endured a cruel enough martyrdom at the foot of the Cross for her Son to spare her all further pain.

It is worth noting that Our Lord delightfully soothed the last moments of those who accompanied Him on Golgotha. Saint John, the only Apostle to follow Him to Calvary, is also the only one not to close his life by a bloody martyrdom.

The thought of death still terrifies us. The recollection of our sins horrifies us. How will the awesome Judge, Whom we have gravely offended so frequently, greet us? The idea of the supreme separation of death devastates us. It will force us to leave behind all the beloved souls to whom so many ties bind us.

If our faith were greater, we would find precious consolation in the teachings of our Religion. True, we have often sinned, but did Our Lord not come to earth for sinners? "For the Son of Man is come to seek and to save that which was lost."[58] Did He not receive guilty sinners with immense pity and infinite tenderness? Did He not pardon Mary Magdalene

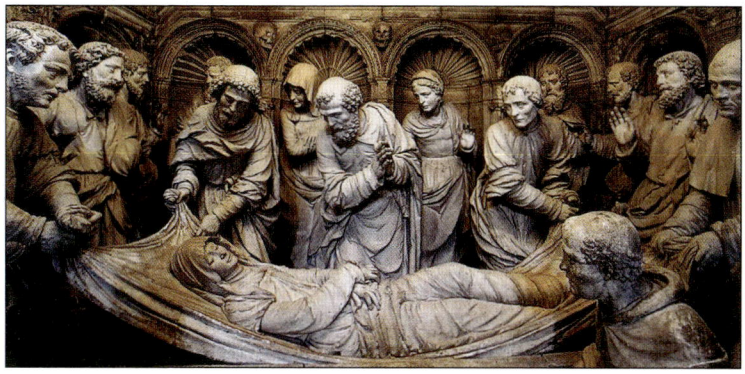

Dormition of the Virgin, Abbey Saint-Pierre, Solesmes, France.

because of her tears of repentance? Did He not protect and convert the unhappy woman whom the Jews had surprised in the very act of her sin? Even more, Our Lord untiringly seeks after the lost sheep until He finds it and brings it back into the fold upon His shoulders, its aching head warmly cradled upon His adorable heart.

Death separates us, but only for a moment. It never breaks the bonds established in the eyes of God. Do you not recite every day those words that sent Saint Thérèse into transports of gratitude: "I believe... in the communion of Saints... the resurrection of the body, and life everlasting?"

Possessing such absolute certitude, how can a Christian fear death? If these truths do not impress upon you great peace, then beg the holy Virgin to enlighten you. She will make you understand a little less poorly the mercy of her Son and the hope of life after death.

* * *

What means did God use to call Our Lady back to Himself? Her Immaculate Conception sheltered her from the humiliating infirmities that overwhelm us in our wretchedness; she could not experience the deterioration of old age, nor the physical lesions of disease.

Her life had been an uninterrupted series of prodigies. By a miracle she had escaped original sin. By a miracle she had conceived the Incarnate Word. By a miracle she had been able to sustain the joys of Divine Motherhood. By a miracle she did not succumb to her martyrdom.

To allow her to die, God had only to suspend the miracle that kept her on earth. Love for her Son consumed her; the desire to join Him burned within her. These emotions depleted her strength. Only the most powerful virtue could sustain her. When her hour came to receive her eternal reward, the Most High had only to suppress this mysterious virtue. Then the ardor of her immense charity overcame her, and the royal soul of the most pure Virgin flew to Heaven upon the wings of her great love.

History records neither the circumstances nor the date of that blessed event. Venerable traditions provide some details which, while not obliging our faith, do stir our piety. The Archangel Gabriel, who had saluted her as "full of grace," visited her anew to announce her departure. A marvelous joy filled her soul.

From that moment, her strength declined rapidly. The Apostles, then providentially gathered in Jerusalem, surrounded the bed where their Mother languished. She blessed them all with her tenderness and promised always to grant the prayers of her children on earth. Then she lifted her eyes to Heaven. Jesus, radiant in His glory, leaned toward her and, in a filial embrace, carried her soul into His eternal kingdom.

After Our Lady exhaled her last breath, the Apostles piously fulfilled the final duties towards her. They buried her according to Jewish custom, laying her, it is believed, in a tomb in the immediate vicinity of Gethsemani.

Death's consequences would not touch this body, sanctified by the true presence of the Incarnate Word. How could corruption dare attack the virginal flesh from which eternal and incorruptible Purity had deigned to be born? The God-Man did not delay in resurrecting His Mother.

How long did Mary's body lay in the tomb? We have no certainty. It is generally thought that Jesus raised her and carried her into Heaven at dawn of the third day after her death, thus further likening His Mother to Himself.

The Coronation of the Blessed Virgin Mary by Fra Angelico.

 The Fathers of the Church have spoken at length about the Immaculate Virgin's triumphant entrance into Heaven. They show her being raised above the angels and saints to heights of glory inaccessible to other creatures. As she arrives before the immortal throne the Savior had prepared for her near His own, the adorable Trinity places upon her forehead the diadem of royalty and proclaims her Queen of the entire universe. Mary receives the treasure of graces merited by her Son's redemptive blood, and she draws abundantly from these heavenly gifts and distributes them according to her incomparable goodness, mercy, and love.

We have often spoken in this work of the power the Mother of Christ possesses in Heaven. Dear reader, you must draw from these meditations the absolute certitude that the Blessed Virgin will never refuse to hear your prayers. She will not hesitate even to work a miracle to grant your requests if such be necessary for your salvation. This is the universal belief of the Church. If you want to be convinced of this, consult the innumerable volumes of the saints and the theologians on the matter.

* * *

Ancient tradition holds that several days after Mary's death, the Apostles, grieving at having lost their Mother, wanted to contemplate her blessed remains one last time. They visited her tomb and drew back the great stone sealing its entrance. Entering the sepulcher, they did not find the body of the Immaculate. On the stone where they had laid her, they found only freshly blooming flowers, whose sweet fragrance delighted and consoled them.

This legend, dating from the first centuries of Christianity, may not bear all the marks of authenticity. Yet it possesses at least a double merit: It attests to the Church's unshakable belief in the Assumption of the Blessed Virgin and it gracefully shows the joys that devotion to our Mother in Heaven gives us.

Preciously safeguard the love of Mary in your heart, and in this heart, at times so anguished, perhaps so guilty, Mary will cause flowers to blossom that will never die.

NOTES

1. John 14:6.
2. John 19:26.
3. Cf. *True Devotion to the Blessed Virgin*, "Fifth Motive for This Devotion."
4. Gabriel Garcia-Moreno, president of Ecuador in the mid-nineteenth century, was martyred for the Faith by Freemasons after receiving Holy Communion. He died in 1875.
5. Ephes. 2:3.
6. *"Pereat dies in qua natus sum, et nox in qua dictum est: conceptus est homo."* (Job 3:3).
7. Canticle of Canticles, 4:7.
8. Saint Bernard. Second sermon on the words of the Gospel "Missus est angelus Gabriel" (The angel Gabriel was sent").
9. Matins, Response after the sixth lesson.
10. Luke 1:66.
11. Isaiah 53:3—"Despised, and the most abject of men, a man of sorrows, and acquainted with infirmity."
12. This work was written prior to the 1950 dogmatic definition of the Assumption, in which Pope Pius XII carefully avoided defining whether the Blessed Virgin experienced a true death or simply a dormition.
13. *"Me reputabam vilissimam et gratia Dei indignam."* Quoted by Saint Alphonsus Liguori in *The Glories of Mary* in discussing her humility.
14. Saint Bernard, *Homilia...super Missus est.*
15. Transl. Note: Fenelon was a priest and writer of the seventeenth century. He is known for his criticism of the political regime of Louis XIV. His Explanations of Maxims of the Saints was condemned by the Church for its quietism. He is nonetheless considered one of France's great thinkers of that time.
16. Matt 26:33-35.
17. Cf. Matt 21:28-32.
18. Homilia 2 super Missus.
19. Canticle of Canticles 4:9.
20. Luke 1:28.
21. Luke 1:30.
22. Luke 1:31-33.
23. Luke 1:34.
24. Luke 1:35-37.
25. Psalm 21:7.
26. Luke 1:38.
27. Matt 1:16 *Jacob autem genuit Joseph, virum Maria de qua natus est Jesus, qui vocatur Christus.*
28. Cf. Saint Epiphanius, *Homil.* 5a in Laud. S. M. V.
29. *"Ad fines divinitatis propria operatione attigit." Summa Theologica,* II-II, q. 103, art 4, ad. 2.
30. Isaiah 1:11.
31. Luke 3:22.
32. Luke 2:51.
33. Luke 17:17.
34. Luke 1:39.
35. John 13:34-35 and 15:12-13.
36. Luke 1:43.
37. Luke 1:46-51.
38. Luke 1:44: *"Exultavit in gaudio infans in utero meo."*
39. Canticle of Canticles 5:2.
40. Luke 6:19: *"Virtus de illo exibat et sanabat omnes."*
41. Matt 9:22.
42. Matt 8:13: *"Sicut credidisti, fiat tibi."*
43. Luke 2:44.
44. Psalm 22:4.
45. Luke 2:48.
46. Luke 2:49.
47. Luke 2:29-30.
48. Luke 2:35.
49. Matt. 27:42.
50. Matt. 27:46.
51. Gen. 21:16.
52. Lam.1:12.
53. Matt. 3:17 and 17:5.
54. Cf. John 12:32.
55. John 19:27.
56. Saint Epiphanius, *Contre les Hérétiques,* Book III, n. 78.
57. See note 12.
58. Luke19:10.